CW00591665

SUPERFAST
AND THE SHIPS OF ATTICA GROUP

Bruce Peter

1

Title page: The port of
Patras in March 2001 with
five members of the
Superfast fleet – from left to
right, the **Superfast IV**, the
newly-delivered Superfast VI,
the **Superfast III**, the
Superfast I and, in the
foreground, the **Superfast V**.
Two much older ferries, the
Erotokritos of Minoan
Lines and the **Agios
Andreas** of Med Link Lines,
are in the middle distance.
(Attica Group)

Ferry
Publications

Published by:
Ferry Publications, PO Box 33,
Ramsey, Isle of Man IM99 4LP

Tel: +44 (0) 1624 898445
Fax: +44 (0) 1624 898449

E-mail: ferrypubs@manx.net
Website: www.ferrypubs.co.uk

CONTENTS

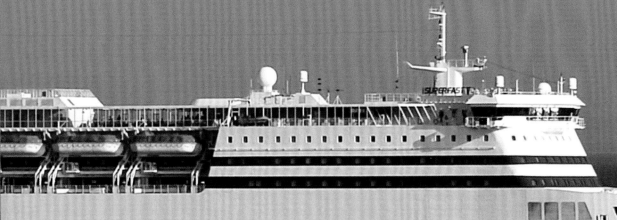

INTRODUCTION

On 4 April 1995, the brand new West German-built ro-pax ferry *Superfast I* set sail from Patras in Greece, bound for Ancona in Italy, launching the first ever regular crossings between the two countries of less than 24 hours' duration. By reducing the voyage time by a third, the *Superfast I* brought Greece closer to the heart of Europe. But Superfast represented so much more than just fast, new ships in an Adriatic ferry market hitherto characterised by slow and old converted vessels, mainly bought second hand from north European operators and from Japan. Superfast was a revolutionary concept in terms of style and branding which caught the lifestyle-orientated spirit of its era. The Superfast concept was subsequently expanded into a network of routes across the Adriatic and in northern Europe – a very rare, unprecedented and so far unique instance of a Greek ferry operator entering the North Sea and Baltic ferry markets. Through the sale of the original Superfast ships on the second hand market, the concept later on spread around the world with its former vessels nowadays found operating in Australia, Canada, the Western Mediterranean, the English Channel, Bay of Biscay, Irish Sea and elsewhere.

When Superfast was launched, the Balkans War was ongoing, meaning that vehicular traffic could no longer travel south and east along former Yugoslavia. In consequence, there was a very rapid growth in ferry traffic over the Adriatic as truckers and tourists alike instead were forced to drive-through Italy and to sail from there to Albania, Greece and Turkey from the ports of Ancona, Bari and Brindisi, all of which experienced major rises in throughput. Mainly Greek shipping entrepreneurs plus some Albanian and Turkish ones too exploited the situation by buying up as many available ferries as could be found at reasonable cost on the second hand market. These often elderly vessels took the best part of two days to make each crossing. Superfast's owner, the Greek shipping tycoon, Pericles Panagopoulos, was persuaded that by considerably speeding up the passage time and using much larger ships comprising large freight decks with boutique hotel-style passenger accommodation and cruise standards of service

Pericles Panagopoulos (centre) with his son, Alexander Panagopoulos (right) and Costis Stamboulelis (left) – three key figures in the creation and development of Superfast. *(Costis Stamboulelis collection)*

on board, the Adriatic ferry market would be revolutionised and this would be to Greece's long-term advantage as it would be 'pulled' closer to the heart of the European Union. Almost twenty-five years later, Panagopoulos's vision of speed and comfort had set a standard emulated by every other ferry operator linking Greece and Italy and the stylish Superfast ships and brand had become famed throughout the industry.

In preparing this book, I am greatly indebted to the naval architect Costis Stamboulelis – Attica Group's Executive Management Adviser for New Buildings & Development – who has served the company and its precursors for 38 years and has overseen all of their new building and conversion projects since the early-1980s. I am also very grateful to the architect and interior designer, Apostolos Molindris, who designed the interiors of most of the Superfast and Blue Star Ferries vessels. Their willingness to assist in placing on record

With dramatic mountains behind, the **Superfast III** approaches Patras in the spring of 2000. *(Bruce Peter)*

the stories of the design, construction and operation of these ships has been invaluable. In addition, I am very grateful to Spiros Paschalis, Chief Executive Officer of Attica Group since 2012, and to Hercules Simitsidellis, Commercial Director of Superfast Ferries 2000-2017, for their assistance in checking the manuscript for its accuracy with regard to commercial developments and for suggesting numerous enhancements, particularly concerning the period since 2000. It is our hope that readers will enjoy learning about the remarkable innovations, risks taken and obstacles overcome to achieve the magnificent fleet of modern ferries operated by Attica Group today.

CHAPTER ONE

PERICLES PANAGOPOULOS'S EARLY CAREER IN SHIPPING

By the time Superfast was launched, Pericles Panagopoulos had accumulated over forty years of shipping industry experience, encompassing the trans-Atlantic passenger liner trades, the cruise business and the operation of bulk carriers and tankers – but not as yet ferries. Self-made and very determined, he had worked hard all his life. He was born in 1935 in Athens but had a tough childhood. His father was an Athens hotelier who had made his first fortune in the United States of America, where he had lived for twenty years from 1907 onwards. When in 1941, Greece was occupied by Nazi Germany, the Gestapo commandeered the Panagopoulos family's hotel for use by its officers, who on one occasion so badly beat up Panagopoulos Senior that he died of his injuries. Young Pericles Panagopoulos, his mother and his two half-brothers from his father's earlier marriage struggled through the remaining war years (in 1944, one of his brothers succumbed to tuberculosis which was rampant in Athens at that time). Fortunately, Panagopoulos's uncle, the Geneva-based Greek ship owner, Eugen Eugenides, who had no children of his own, took a close interest in young Pericles, bringing him to Switzerland and paying for his education there. Greece was badly damaged by the Second World War, which was followed by a civil war between

The lighthouse at the port of Bari in Italy, as viewed from the *Superfast II* at the commencement of a crossing of the Adriatic. *(Bruce Peter)*

Communists – who wished the country to align with the Soviet sphere of influence – and those who preferred it to align with the West. This lasted until 1949, during which period many Greeks emigrated to begin new lives in the Americas and in Australia. As neutral Switzerland was largely unaffected by the wartime chaos and carnage in neighbouring countries, for the first time in Panagopoulos's life since very early childhood, he experienced relative comfort and security during these years.

Just like Panagopoulos's mother, Eugen Eugenides had spent his formative years in Constantinople where his first business experience was as an importer of Swedish timber; this first brought him into contact with the large Gothenburg-headquartered Broström shipping group which, in addition to a substantial fleet of general cargo ships, owned the famous Swedish-American Line which operated glamorous white-painted trans-Atlantic liners. Eugenides spent the Second World War in Argentina and when peace returned, he became one of the first Greek ship owners to enter the international liner trades, rather than focusing on tramp shipping, as was the case with the majority. In addition to his Greek South American Line freight service, in 1948 he formed a joint company with Broströms and with the Cosulich Line of Trieste, called 'Home Lines' (the name being an English derivation of the Swedish 'Holm' which was the suffix of the names of the Swedish-American passenger ships). This was in response to the need to transport a wave of westbound emigrants, consisting mainly of displaced Germans and impoverished Italians seeking to begin new lives in the Americas. To transport these migrants, a Home Lines subsidiary company took over the former Norwegian America Liner *Bergensfjord* of 1913, which was renamed the *Argentina* in 1946 and placed in migrant service between Genoa and South American ports, flying the Panamanian flag. Subsequently, two of the older members of the Swedish-American Line fleet, the *Drottningholm* of 1904 and the *Kungsholm* of 1928, were added to the fleet, renamed the *Brasil* and the *Italia* respectively, the latter in addition operating a budget UK-Canada service.

Eugenides, meanwhile, had sent Panagopoulos for further education in business administration at the École Supérieure de Commerce in Lausanne. After a period back in Greece, he was next dispatched by Eugenides to London, who in common with many Greek ship owners also had an office there in which Panagopoulos was henceforth employed. At the same time, he attended evening classes at the City of London College to learn shipping law. Along the way, he became fluent in French, Italian and English. These achievements suggest that Panagopoulos was both a bright young man and a prodigious worker. During the university summer recess, Eugenides put him to work at sea aboard his cargo liners and on the Home Lines passenger ships so that he would also learn at first-hand about as many aspects of the practicalities of day-to-day ship operation as possible. Although only in his mid-teens, he had to 'muck in' with the crew. As he subsequently recalled, when serving on Eugenides' cargo ships, 'I found myself in Middle East in times of war and I was in Jerusalem [in 1951] when King Abdullah of Jordan was assassinated. It was unbelievable!'

In 1954, Eugen Eugenidis died suddenly and, for Panagopoulos, his passing brought to an abrupt end a vital relationship. In the following year, Panagopoulos was moved by Eugenides' successors from London to Home Lines' Geneva headquarters where, except during national service in the Greek Army, he remained until marrying in 1962. Thereafter, he returned to London as Head of Home Lines' British Sales and Reservations Department, which fed its trans-Atlantic route between Britain and Canada. This was a declining trade, however, and due to the rise of jet air travel was closed down within less than a year of Panagopoulos's arrival. Next, he was sent to Monfalcone in Italy as Home Lines' superintendent to oversee the construction of a new and sophisticated cruise ship, the

Home Lines' emigrant liner ***Brasil***, formerly the Swedish ***Drottningholm*** of 1904, was among the first passenger ships with which Pericles Panagopoulos was involved. *(Bruce Peter collection)*

Oceanic, for operation year-round between New York and the Caribbean. In terms of design and layout, the vessel proved to be one of the most advanced and prophetic of the many diverse passenger ships built during the 1960s and in service was a tremendous and enduring success – but for Panagopoulos personally, the project caused a great deal of stress as the shipyard's management was in turmoil and costs increased beyond what had been expected. When the *Oceanic* was completed in 1965, Panagopoulos resigned from Home Lines and returned to Greece.

Back in Athens, he had few shipping industry connections, partly as a result of not personally belonging to any of the existing Greek shipping dynasties, which tended to employ family members, and of having worked elsewhere in the world for nearly all of his career to date. After several rejections, he eventually was hired by the cruise ship entrepreneur, Haralambos Kiosceoglou, who like Panagopoulos had begun his career as an employee of Home Lines under Eugen Eugenides but who left in the mid-1950s to found his own cruise company, which he named simply Sun Line. His initial vessel was

The *Italia* of Home Lines, formerly the **Kungsholm** of 1928, passes through the Dover Strait. *(FotoFlite)*

identical vessels presented to Greece and war reparations and known on account of their names as 'the Love ships' (the others were the *Eros* and *Adonis*). The vessels' initial owner, the Hellenic Tourism Association, quickly sold them on to Greek cruise operators and all were rebuilt as cruise ships. Following conversion, the *Aphrodite* was renamed *Stella Oceanis*.

Pericles Panagopoulos had a central role in the development of Sun Line in the second half of the 1960s and, by the end of the decade, the company was expanding its horizons beyond the Aegean with the purchase in 1970 from the French liner company, Messageries Maritimes, of a much larger steam turbine-powered passenger and cargo liner, the 13,217grt *Cambodge* of 1953, which hitherto had operated between Marseille and the Far East. Kiosceoglou planned to rebuild her substantially into a luxury cruise ship, the *Stella Solaris* (II), for Mediterranean and Caribbean operation – but the work required was so extensive that it took three years to complete.

converted in 1958 from a British Royal Navy frigate, HMS *Hespeler*, into the cruise ship *Stella Maris* which he used successfully on Greek island itineraries. Next, in 1962, Kiosceoglou purchased the five-year-old, 2,520 grt West German excursion ship *Bunte Kuh*, which had been built by the Norderwerft in Hamburg, from the Hamburg-based Hafen-Dampfschiffahrt-Actien-Gesellschaft. Hitherto, the vessel had provided day-long cruises down the River Elbe to Cuxhaven and onward to the island of Helgoland in the North Sea. Upon arrival in Greece, she was rebuilt with the addition of *en suite* cabins, emerging in the spring of 1963 as the Aegean cruise ship *Stella Solaris*.

Kiosceoglou's third cruise ship was acquired in 1965 and was also a West German-built day excursion vessel, the *Bremerhaven* of 1960, which became the *Stella Maris II*, replacing his original ship of that name. Next, Kiosceoglou bought a newly-completed Italian-built stern loading car ferry, the 3,963grt *Aphrodite*, which was one of three

In the interim, Panagopoulos decided that, rather than remaining with Sun Line, he would develop his own cruise company and, instead of converting second hand tonnage as was the typical approach of Greek cruise ship and ferry operators at that time, he would instead commission a purpose-built vessel. This was a very bold move which set him on a unique course as Greece's leading innovator in passenger shipping. Thus, having learned a great deal about the cruise industry from Kiosceoglou, the two parted company in 1971 and, thereafter, Panagopoulos set about advancing this ambitious new project.

The Sun Line cruise ship **Stella Solaris**, ex-**Cambodge**, at Santorini in the mid-1970s. *(Bruce Peter collection)*

Home Lines' innovative **Oceanic** in the construction of which Pericles Panagopoulos was involved as a superintendent. *(Bruce Peter collection)*

The small Sun Line cruise ship **Stella Oceani**s, which was converted from the modern Italian-built car ferry **Aphrodite**. *(Bruce Peter collection)*

CHAPTER TWO

ROYAL CRUISE LINE

Organising a new cruise line from scratch was a daunting task, requiring first a detailed business plan to convince enough financiers to have faith in investing in it. The task was all the more challenging as the amount of money required to build a new cruise ship was far greater than buying at close to scrap value and converting an old ferry or liner would have been (as had happened with the *Cambodge* to *Stella Solaris* project).

Although intending to operate among the islands of the Aegean Sea, Panagopoulos took inspiration for his concept from the success of Norwegian-owned cruise lines running week-long Caribbean fly-cruises from Miami. Panagopoulos's plan was to fly planeloads of Americans to Athens, from which they would be transferred to his cruise ship in Piraeus. Middle-aged, middle class Americans represented by far the largest clientele in the global cruise market at that time but it was relatively difficult for them to get to the Mediterranean. By developing tie-ins with airlines already linking US cities with Athens, it would be possible to bring over whole shiploads on a weekly basis.

The first of the Norwegian-owned Caribbean cruise fleets was Norwegian Caribbean Line (NCL), owned by Knut Kloster of the Lauritz Kloster Rederi of Oslo. In the second half of the 1960s, it had first introduced cruises from Miami to the Bahamas and Jamaica using newly-built vessels, the designs of which were derived from those of typical Scandinavian overnight ferries of the same era. The NCL ships were thus highly efficient in terms of high passenger density, fuel economy and ability to be turned around in Miami in only a few hours.

In particular, the newly-created Royal Caribbean Cruise Line appeared to have a business model that appeared to Panagopoulos to be well worth emulating in terms of image, branding, market penetration, quality level, style of ships and operational organisation. Its name sounded aspirational and its logo – consisting of a crown and anchor – was clear and reinforced the link between the idea of royalty and that of maritime tradition (besides, it appeared that anything with a 'royal' prefix would be a commercial success in the USA). Royal Caribbean was at that time inaugurating three state-of-

the-art purpose-built cruise ships, the *Song of Norway*, *Nordic Prince* and *Sun Viking*, all of which were built in Finland by the Wärtsilä shipyard in Helsinki. In terms of size, style and facilities, they were slightly upmarket of the rival NCL fleet but likewise derived from Scandinavian ferry design precedents in terms of propulsion, hull design and the organisation of service flows for provisions. In terms of company structure, both NCL and Royal Caribbean were ultimately managed from Oslo but their cruise sales and day-to-day operations were organised from offices in Miami. Panagopoulos decided to follow a similar approach, splitting management activities between the owning nation, Greece, and the principal market, the USA. The initial designs for both the NCL and Royal Caribbean ships had been drawn up by the Danish consulting naval architects, Knud E. Hansen A/S, and it was to their Copenhagen office that Panagopoulos headed to commission a design for his cruise ship; with this created, he would be able to invite tenders from potential builders. Meanwhile, he would also need to find a way of financing the project.

At that time, a prominent and well-connected Norwegian shipping manager, Eric Heirung, who was managing director of Fred. Olsen Lines, had been asked by a Danish shipyard, Helsingør Skibsværft, which was a subsidiary of the DFDS shipping company, to act as a consultant to help it to win new contracts. Panagopoulos had a chance encounter with Heirung, who suggested to him that the Helsingør yard would be ideal to build the proposed cruise ship. Heirung even proposed to DFDS that they might become a partner in the project and provide a large amount of the necessary finance. DFDS refused, however; it considered itself to be a liner and ferry company and had no interest in operating cruise ships, especially not in partnership with an unknown Greek entrepreneur. Nonetheless, Panagopoulos succeeded in raising the required capital alone.

Panagopoulos's extensive experience of the passenger shipping industry from his periods of employment with Home Lines and Sun Line meant that he had a great deal of first-hand expertise which he now put to good use in the designing of his 'perfect' cruise ship. The planning of the vessel – to be named the *Golden Odyssey*, reflecting

Royal Cruise Line's **Golden Odyssey** was Pericles Panagopoulos's pride and joy – and the finest ship of the 1970s in the Greek cruising fleet. Here, the vessel is seen at Hydra, one of the small ports at which Royal Cruise Line initially called. *(Attica Group)*

A stairway on the **Golden Odyssey** with an abstract mural by Michaelis Katzourakis on the bulkhead. *(Bruce Peter collection)*

The bright and fresh-looking Calypso nightclub with another Katzourakis panel behind the bar. *(Bruce Peter collection)*

Homer's ancient epic – was mainly developed by the naval architect, Tage Wandborg, of Knud E. Hansen A/S. Wandborg had previously designed all of the Norwegian Caribbean fleet and had also been involved in designing Royal Caribbean's vessels, working jointly with their Finnish builder. He was therefore one of the leading experts in cruise ship design at that time. In addition, he was a considerable aesthete whose solutions were very futuristic-looking, yet with harmonious details. In a north European context, Wandborg was also an innovator in his preference for the use of American-style fire-proof materials for ship interiors (as opposed to the woodwork traditionally preferred for these in Britain and Scandinavia).

In terms of overall layout, Wandborg's *Golden Odyssey* design was in many respects a smaller version of the new Royal Caribbean ships, having most of the public rooms filling the full width of a single saloon deck with cabins on the decks below within the hull and also above, inboard of the lifeboats. Measuring 9,848 grt – half the size of the Royal Caribbean sisters – the capacity for 509 passengers was nonetheless only a couple of hundred berths less theirs, reflecting Panagopoulos's desire that it would be optimised to accommodate a single wide-bodied jet-load. Tage Wandborg recalls that Panagopoulos was 'the best client I ever had… he had a good eye for every detail and was very diligent in reviewing the plans and making good suggestions to improve them.' One of Wandborg's naval architect colleagues, Hans Kjærgaard, who also was heavily involved in the project, remembers how Panagopoulos wanted cabins re-arranged to make the best use of space and spotted several locations on the initial layout drawings where, with some re-arrangement, an extra cabin could be fitted in.

At the superstructure's aft end, the decks were tiered around a lido area and another of these was located between the mast and funnel, both areas being sheltered by curved glazed screens. The bow had very pronounced sheer and the funnel had a large smoke-deflecting fin, balancing the profile. From a distance, the overall impression was of a very large white-painted motor yacht. Royal Cruise Line's logo was a golden crown and this was displayed on the prow and on either side of the funnel casing.

Inboard, the *Golden Odyssey* was technologically a state-of-the-art

Top: Having transferred to the American West Coast, the **Golden Odyssey** is seen leaving Vancouver in the late-1970s. *(Bruce Peter collection)*.

Left: The **Golden Odyssey** at Vancouver in the late-1980s, by which time the vessel had developed a superb reputation in the demanding North American market. *(Bruce Peter collection)*

vessel, being fully air conditioned to tropical specifications and all cabins had private bathrooms. The interiors were designed jointly by Wandborg and a Greek abstract artist whom Panagopoulos employed called Michalis Katzourakis, who subsequently widened his career to specialise additionally in designing cruise ship interiors. For the *Golden Odyssey*, he produced a series of large abstract mural panels to adorn the stairwells and the bulkheads of the main public rooms. Otherwise, the décor and furnishing were distinctly Nordic, Wandborg and Katzourakis choosing chairs by Eero Saarinen, Arne Jacobsen and other famous modern architects and designers.

Upon completion in 1974, the *Golden Odyssey* was widely praised as being among the finest passenger ships ever built in Denmark; everything that could possibly have been done to ensure the vessel's success had been attended to. What neither Panagopoulos nor the ship's designers and builders foresaw, unfortunately, was the 1973 Oil Crisis which resulted from Arab oil producing nations slashing production of Gulf crude in protest at American and other western support for Israel in the Yom Kippur War. Consequently, when the *Golden Odyssey* was delivered, the cost of oil had quadrupled, meaning that the expense of flying passengers from the USA to Greece had risen sharply and the price of bunker oil to power ships' engines was also much more than had been budgeted. Moreover, the value of the dollar fell sharply, then fluctuated unpredictably, meaning that it was impossible to predict how much cash-flow there would be in terms of earnings and overheads.

Just before the Oil Crisis, while the *Golden Odyssey*'s construction was advancing, Panagopoulos had been working with Knud E. Hansen A/S's naval architects and with the Helsingør Shipyard on plans for a second, somewhat larger, cruise ship. As Panagopoulos found it difficult to raise enough capital, and as the shipyard strongly desired a follow-on order to maintain continuity of employment, it put together a financial package, raising the necessary equity mostly from Danish investors. Panagopoulos evidently had growing anxieties about the viability of the project as, only a short time before the contract signing ceremony was due to take place, he abruptly cancelled these scheme – a pragmatic decision given the very unpredictable economic situation at that time.

To sell his Mediterranean cruises in the American market, Panagopoulos established a sales organisation in San Francisco. To lead this, he was fortunate in appointing a very dynamic Executive Vice President, Richard Revnes – a well-known travel trade and airline entrepreneur from the Mid-West. During the Second World War, he had served as a pilot in the US Airforce and gave the impression of being fearless even when faced with daunting

challenges. His thorough knowledge of American travel sales and marketing would prove crucial for the success of the Royal Cruise Line project.

As the *Golden Odyssey*'s initial Aegean season had not proved as lucrative as had been hoped, Revnes made the bold suggestion that instead the vessel should be re-located to the US West Coast to sail from San Francisco and Vancouver. That way, passengers would only need to pay for domestic flights, rather than long-haul international ones.

Revnes personally fronted Royal Cruise Line's advertising campaign and appeared in its brochures to reassure American passengers that the operation was an ideal combination of American managerial organisation and Greek seamanship and hospitality – and

The newly-converted **Royal Odyssey** arrives at the port of New York in the autumn of 1982. *(Attica Group)*

that, although relatively expensive and upmarket, its cruises actually offered good value for money. On board, Royal Cruise Line's attention to detail was fastidious and the mix of Greek and European cuisine served in the dining room was particularly well received, while the officers and hotel staff were notable for their warmth and courtesy. The outcome of these efforts was a tremendous success with the *Golden Odyssey* now sailing full to capacity week after week. Indeed, the vessel gained a formidable reputation, becoming a West Coast equivalent of Home Lines' popular *Oceanic*, which cruised from New York. (Many of the details of Royal Cruise Lines' service provision were based upon what Panagopoulos had learned from Home Lines and from Sun Line). Very important for any successful cruise line was the number of repeat passengers attracted – and in this respect, Royal Cruise Line's fine reputation and competitive fares enabled it quickly to gain a substantial and loyal following.

All the while, Panagopoulos kept Knud E. Hansen A/S's naval architects employed, developing and refining new cruise ship concepts. The question for him was when the American and Western economy would feel sufficiently stable to invest in a second vessel. In the end, however, Panagopoulos decided that it would be less risky and more cost-effective to buy on the second hand market, then to convert, as was more the Greek tradition. An opportunity arose in the early-1980s when Home Lines decided to replace its secondary cruise ship, the 25,338 grt *Doric*, which operated from New York alongside the *Oceanic*, with a new building. As Panagopoulos already had a distant business relationship with Home Lines' owners, the Eugenides family, he negotiated to buy the *Doric* and to take delivery when the latter company's replacement vessel, the *Atlantic*, entered service in 1982.

The *Doric* had had a relatively complex history, Panagopoulos being its fourth owner in just 18 years. The vessel was a turbine steamer, rather than a motor ship like the *Golden Odyssey*, and had been delivered in 1964 by Chantiers de l'Atlantique at St Nazaire in France for trans-Atlantic liner service as the *Shalom*, owned by the Zim Lines of Haifa in Israel. She was not a success, however, a situation attributable both to the rapid rise of long-haul jet air travel and to the fact that the her cuisine was exclusively kosher, which meant she was less attractive for non-Jewish passengers. Zim Lines therefore sold her in 1968 to the Deutsche Atlantik Linie of Hamburg for use as a cruise ship, named the *Hanseatic*. When Deutsche Atlantik ran out of money and gave up operations around the time of the 1973 Oil Crisis, Home Lines bought her to supplement its highly successful *Oceanic*.

Panagopoulos commissioned a conversion plan from Knud E. Hansen A/S from which the *Doric* would emerge, so far as passengers were concerned, as a 'new' ship named the *Royal Odyssey* and with fresh interiors designed by Michalis Katzourakis in a style similar to those of the Golden Odyssey. Even her original twin smoke stacks were replaced with a single conical-shaped funnel, thereby giving her a new profile. This work was to be carried out over the 1981-82 winter at Perama in Greece – a district of the Piraeus/Athens conurbation where many shipyards are located – and at the Neorion shipyard on the island of Syros.

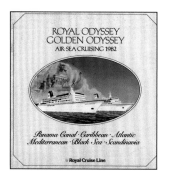

Converting an existing ship, however, can reveal unexpected problems and the *Doric*-to-*Royal Odyssey* project was no exception. As Tage Wandborg subsequently recalled:

'I surveyed the *Doric* for Panagopoulos and found her to be a fine vessel – although when she pitched in a head sea, there was a strange shuddering which at first I could not explain. When she was dry-docked in Perama, it was found that the stem of her bow was not exactly straight and, remarkably, this was actually the result of a collision she had suffered when brand new as the *Shalom* she had collided with an oil tanker on the Hudson River. The repairs carried out were less than perfect and so, ever since, she had sailed with this misalignment.'

The opportunity was thus taken fit a new stem with an improved bulbous bow. Royal Cruise Line's newly-appointed Superintendent Naval Architect, Costis Stamboulelis, oversaw the rebuilding work on behalf of the owner. As we shall see, Stamboulelis – who was a graduate in Naval Architecture of Sunderland Polytechnic and of the University of Michigan and most recently had been employed by the Technical University of Athens – would go on to occupy key roles in Panagopoulos's shipping companies and would supervise the development of all of their subsequent vessels.

The converted *Royal Odyssey* entered service in the summer of 1982 and operated not only in the Mediterranean but also in northern Europe and even in the Pacific – two new spheres of operations for Royal Cruise Line.

Soon Panagopoulos began working with Knud E. Hansen A/S on a project for a further purpose-built cruise ship, on this occasion substantially bigger than either the *Golden Odyssey* or *Royal Odyssey*. In the 1980s, the cruise industry experienced substantial growth, mainly in the USA but also with sales increasing in Europe. At the same time, a new generation of larger and better appointed cruise ships was entering service, arguably the most outstanding of which in terms of innovative concepts was P&O Princess Cruises' *Royal Princess*, which was delivered in 1984 from the Finnish shipbuilder, Wärtsilä. Among the vessel's many novel features were a layout with only outside cabins and all technical services arranged in casings along the centreline, plus many cabins with their own private balconies. These characteristics were emulated in the new Royal Cruise Line ship, which was designed largely by Tage Wandborg of Knud E. Hansen A/S who worked closely with Pericles Panagopoulos and Costis Stamboulelis. (In 1985 Stamboulelis was appointed as Royal Cruise Line's New Building Project Manager.) The plan was that the vessel would replace the *Royal Odyssey* which, being a turbine steamship, was far less fuel efficient and therefore also much less profitable than purpose-built diesel-powered cruise vessels.

Eventually, after much discussion between client and naval architects and the production of numerous plans and revisions, in 1985, Royal Cruise Line placed an order with Meyer Werft at Papenburg, which at that time had under construction a large enclosed building dock created with the specific intention of building cruise ships. The new Royal Cruise Line vessel, to be named the *Crown Odyssey*, would be the first vessel to be floated out from this facility, rather than launched sideways as had been the case at the

Michaelis Katzourakis was responsible for designing new interiors for the ***Royal Odyssey***. Here, we see part of the liner's Odyssey Lounge. *(Bruce Peter collection)*

The card room on the ***Royal Odyssey*** with a Katzourakis artwork on the bulkhead. *(Bruce Peter collection)*

The ***Royal Odyssey***'s Calypso Lounge; it will be evident that the vessel provided a generous amount of space in which to relax. *(Bruce Peter collection)*

The brand new German-built **Crown Odyssey** navigates slowly through the murky waters of the Panama Canal in the late-1980s. *(Attica Group)*

yard until then.

Measuring 34,242 gt and accommodating up to 1,203 passengers, the *Crown Odyssey* was superbly appointed and with a very high-level of fit, finish and detailing – characteristics of Panagopoulos's, Katzourakis's and Stamboulelis's methods of working and of Meyer Werft's very progressive approach to ship construction. Following Tage Wandborg's retirement from Knud E. Hansen A/S, one of his colleagues, Holger Terpet, who had been employed by the firm since the early-1960s, assisted with detailed design work and the supervision of the construction process. As we shall see, Terpet subsequently became a significant figure in the development of the Superfast ferry concept.

Inboard, the *Crown Odyssey* was much glitzier than the two earlier Royal Cruise Line ships had been. All of the penthouse cabins on the topmost accommodation deck had private balconies while those on the deck below had bay windows, giving angled views forward and aft. Again, Michalis Katzourakis was responsible for the interior design but, on this occasion, his approach was very much in a contemporary American luxury hotel idiom, making extensive use of marble, granite, polished brass and mirrored surfaces; this was, after all, the era in which the soap opera 'Dynasty' was an international television hit.

When the *Crown Odyssey* entered service in 1988, the cruise industry was entering a phase of consolidation. Smaller operators such as Royal Cruise Line were unable to match the rate of expansion of larger ones, such as the Miami-based Carnival Cruise Line, which in 1987 had been listed on the New York Stock Exchange. The *Crown Odyssey* had cost 178 million US dollars to build – a very large sum – but by the late-1980s, cruise ships were on order that were twice her size. Pericles Panagopoulos therefore decided in 1989 to sell his business to another of the expanding future cruise industry giants, Kloster Cruise International, which was the parent company of the Norwegian operators, Norwegian Caribbean Line and Royal Viking Line. As Costis Stamboulelis recollects,

'The sale of Royal Cruise Line was concluded while the *Crown Odyssey* was having its first dry-docking at Neorion Shipyard of Syros. When this was done, the ship returned to Piraeus and I disembarked for the last time. The Greek flag had been replaced by that of the Bahamas and a couple of painters were painting over the original port of registry at the stern. I was very unhappy and must have looked like it because when I was entering the office building Mr. Panagopoulos was coming out of the elevator and, seeing me, he took me aside and said "Cheer up Costis, this is not the end. I am not going to start selling shoes now; we will go back to the sea and shipping!"'

Royal Cruise Line's subsequent history was far from happy, however; although Kloster switched ships to it from other brands, without Panagopoulos and his long-serving Greek and American senior managers to oversee operations, the company lost its sense of direction and unique identity. Perhaps too the cultural differences between Greek ways of doing things and Norwegian ones were too great. (Subsequently, in the early-1990s, when Carnival Cruise Line invested in another well-established Greek cruise business, Epirotiki Line, the outcome was also far from harmonious.) In 1996, Kloster abandoned the Royal Cruise Line brand altogether and two of its ships were reallocated to the NCL fleet. By that time, Pericles Panagopoulos had re-emerged as a major player in the Adriatic ferry business. The story of how this happened will be related in the following chapters.

The ***Crown Odyssey***'s Yacht Club nightclub, with an illuminated dance floor; to address the taste of Royal Cruise Line's predominantly American clientele, Michaelis Katzourakis's approach had changed considerably since his initial work on the ***Golden Odyssey*** 15 years previously. *(Bruce Peter collection)*

The glitzy atrium of the ***Crown Odyssey***, which featured a large amount of lacquered brass and, adjacent to the stairs, a sculpture of a fractured sphere by Arnaldo Pomodoro. *(Bruce Peter collection)*

The Monte Carlo Court lounge on the ***Crown Odyssey***. *(Bruce Peter collection)*

CHAPTER THREE

PANAGOPOULOS'S NEW PLANS

When Pericles Panagopoulos sold Royal Cruise Line to Kloster, a condition of the sale was that he must not be involved in the cruise business for a period of five years. At that time, Panagopoulos was planning to work on developing a new cruise line to be launched once the embargo had ended. He therefore kept employed his key financial managers and his New Building Project Manager, Costis Stamboulelis.

Early in 1990 Panagopoulos and Stamboulelis contacted the naval architects, Knud E. Hansen A/S, to commission plans for a new generation of cruise ship with 2,500 lower berths, the initial intention being to develop the design so that an order could be placed with delivery in 1994, just after the Kloster embargo would end. Panagopoulos, meanwhile, contacted the owners of Sun Line, the Kiosceoglou family, to find out if they might sell the company to him so that it would become the operator of his new vessels. The fact that it was already well-known and had a good international reputation made such a deal attractive from Panagopoulos's point of view – but instead Sun Line's owners opted to merge with another established Greek cruise ship operator, Epirotiki Line, to form Royal Olympic Cruises.

Another idea for a new cruise project came from Gerasimos Strintzis, the main owner of the Adriatic and Aegean ferry operator Strintzis Lines, who in 1990 proposed forming a joint company with Panagopoulos to convert radically a second hand Japanese ferry he had just bought into a cruise ship. The vessel in question was the 11,880 grt *Ishikari*, which had been built in 1974 by Nakai Zozen for Taiheyo Ferry. As much of the vessel's internal volume was given over to freight decks, any rebuilding would be complex and costly and so Strintzis and Panagopoulos decided not to pursue the idea and instead Strintzis sold the vessel to Minoan Lines which subsequently operated it with relatively little modification on Adriatic ferry routes for over a decade as the *Erotokritos*.

Meanwhile, Panagopoulos decided to invest some of his earnings from the Royal Cruise Line sale in the potentially lucrative deep-sea dry bulk shipping business and so in 1991 he established a new

company, Magna Marine, for which he purchased the Japanese-built 45,244 dwt Panamax bulk carrier *Antzouletta* of 1978, which was renamed *Panacea*. Magna Marine's funnel logo consisted of four blue letter 'P's, arranged in the shape of a ship's propeller, and this was designed by Michalis Katzourakis. Subsequently, Magna Marine bought several other second hand Panamax bulk carriers. Bulk shipping is very different from the cruise business; in the tramping trade, vessels are routed to wherever in the world there is a cargo requiring shipping and, quite often, they are bought and sold whenever the market changes, or a profitable sales opportunity appears. In the era since the Second World War, Greek ship owners became highly adept at judging market changes and buying or selling whenever most propitious. The fact that they were small, tightly-managed organisations meant that it was easier to respond quickly to opportunities than in large shareholder companies, in which it was first necessary to receive approval from an executive board. Unusually in a market dominated by flag of convenience tonnage, all of the Magna vessels flew the Greek flag; indeed, the highly patriotic Panagopoulos never countenanced the use any other for any of his shipping ventures.

In January 1992 Panagopoulos purchased Attica Flour Mills, a dormant company which had been founded in 1918 as the General Company of Commerce and Industry of Greece and which had a listing on the Athens Stock Exchange; this he renamed Attica Enterprises with the intention of using it as a means by which to raise capital for investment in a range of hopefully lucrative businesses.

By the year's end, Attica Enterprises had made its first acquisitions, namely the yacht chartering company Vernicos Yachts Shipping, Akron-Ilion – an Athens-based manufacturer and retailer of crystal, glass and tableware – plus a significant shareholding in the Hellenic Register of Shipping and, of particular relevance to this narrative, an initial investment was made in the Greek ferry shipping sector. This was achieved through the purchase of a 17.6 per cent shareholding in Strintzis Lines, the company with which Panagopoulos had recently considered forming a joint cruise line venture. The shareholding was sold back to Strintzis about one year later, however, when Strintzis Lines was listed on the Athens Stock Exchange.

At around this point, Pericles Panagopoulos was contacted by the Italian shipyard Societa Esercizio Cantieri of Viareggio which was looking for a client willing to try out an unusual design of so-called 'surface effect ship' or 'SES' it had been developing. This combined twin hulls like a catamaran, capable of supporting the entire weight of the vessel when in port, with a hovercraft-like air cushion to lift the hulls up to the water's surface and thereby reduce resistance and drag to a minimum when at sea. The origins of this hybrid fast craft type could be traced back to the early-1960s when experiments were carried out by the US Navy and its prototype had reached speeds of over 60 knots on trials. Subsequently, in the 1970s and 80s, other developers had produced their own versions. Societa Esercizio Cantieri's design was for a small passenger-only craft, the profile of which was styled by the famous automotive bodywork specialist, Giorgetto Giugiaro. According to Costis Stamboulelis, he and Panagopoulos were given a personal tour of Giugiaro's studio and exhibition hall when they visited it along with senior managers from Societa Esercizio Cantieri. Panagopoulos thought that the SES design could be used on the Aegean to provide a superior level of fast domestic inter-island passenger services, competing effectively with a fleet of Soviet-built 'Kometa'-type hydrofoils operated by Ceres Flying Dolphins, among others. On this basis, Societa Esercizio Cantieri commissioned model tests of its SES design at the Swedish State Shipbuilding Experimentation Tank (SSPA) in Gothenburg. Although these demonstrated its potential and discussions with the yard reached a point where Panagopoulos's lawyer became involved to discuss contract terms, Panagopoulos decided that it was too risky to proceed to the placement of an order as there remained many areas of technical uncertainty and concerns about the design's commercial viability. (In the end, Societa Esercizio Cantieri never succeeded in building any surface effect ships.)

Subsequently, Panagopoulos and Stamboulelis were introduced to Max Martin, an Australian designer and salesman of fast catamarans. Martin believed that Greece would be an ideal new market for such craft as the economies of its many islands would benefit from shortened passage times to and from the mainland ports. Panagopoulos and Stamboulelis thought that Martin's concepts were very interesting and that the craft he was offering might indeed be highly appropriate for a new type of Greek domestic ferry operation from Piraeus or Rafina to some of the Aegean islands, most likely the central Cyclades. There, as on the Adriatic, existing services were

provided by ageing conventional ferries bought second hand from northern Europe and Japan and incapable of speeds of much more than 20 knots. In addition, the 'Kometa' passenger-only hydrofoils which operated on some shorter routes had cramped interiors resembling aircraft cabins and gave a very bumpy and noisy ride. By contrast, the designs Martin was offering would be smooth, very spacious and relatively quiet inboard, as well as being able to carry substantial payloads of cars and freight. Stamboulelis assessed the advantages and disadvantages of various options for catamarans and monohulls but, on balance, he considered that a 94-metre-long Austal catamaran design with a 42-knot speed would be most ideal for Aegean routes. Stamboulelis recalls that Panagopoulos quickly came to believe that such operations could indeed constitute a successful new shipping business, although such a project entailed certain commercial and technical risks. For example, at that time, the

In the ealy-1990s, Adriatic ferry services were provided by a wide diversity of older vessels, many operated by small companies. The **Crown M.** of Marlines, seen here at Ancona, was originally Fred. Olsen's **Black Watch** of 1966 and was among the more luxurious ships in the Greece-Italy trade. *(Bruce Peter)*

High-Speed Code for the specification and classification of fast ferries was only under development.

Nonetheless, Panagopoulos and Stamboulelis visited the Austal shipyard in Perth, where they reached agreement on all the points in the specification documents and even commenced contract negotiations. Stamboulelis recalls that 'the deal did not go through because at the last moment the Australians declared they could not accept the tight margin of error demanded by Panagopoulos's side for deficiency in speed. Panagopoulos then said that he was only

The most established of the incumbent Greek ferry operators providing services across the Adriatic to Italy was Hellenic Mediterranean Lines, whose old-fashioned and slow *Poseidonia* was originally the P&O Irish Sea ferry *Ulster Queen*. *(Bruce Peter)*

prepared to assume the commercial risk of the catamaran project if the yard would assume the technical risk, otherwise there would be no deal. The Australians were afraid and that was the end of that.' (Around a decade later, fast Austal catamarans of the type Panagopoulos had nearly ordered were being bought by other Greek domestic ferry operators and they did indeed prove highly successful.)

In parallel with these ventures, Panagopoulos, Stamboulelis and Knud E. Hansen A/S continued to develop plans for a large purpose-built cruise ship so as to re-enter the cruise industry in the mid-1990s. They developed it to the extent that in January 1991 bids were invited from various potential builders. The last to be submitted was from the famous French builder, Chantiers de l'Atlantique of St Nazaire. Like all the other bids, it was deemed too high – indeed, to build the ship would have cost more than Panagopoulos had earned through the Royal Cruise Line sale. Costis Stamboulelis recalls what happened next:

'It was an exorbitant offer and a big blow to our plans. Having discussed the French offer with Mr. Panagopoulos, Jean Bernard Raoust, our shipbroker, came to my office and asked me what I thought about it. I said that although I did not have the entrepreneurial mind of Mr. Panagopoulos I could not figure out why paying practically the whole amount of the sale of Royal Cruise Line for just one ship would make sense. Apparently it did not make sense to Mr. Panagopoulos either

and, disappointing as it must have been for him, the project was abandoned.'

Stamboulelis, however, spotted an opportunity to plant in Panagopoulos's mind a radical alternative idea. Back in 1988 when the cruise ship *Crown Odyssey* was nearing completion at Meyer Werft in West Germany, Stamboulelis – who had stayed at the shipyard as project manager for two years and had bought a new car – drove it home to Greece. This meant crossing the Adriatic Sea by ferry, the vessel being Minoan Lines' 10,164 grt, 18-knot *King Minos*, which had originally been built for Japanese coastal service in 1972 as the *Erimo Maru*. The fact that the crossing took over 30 hours led Stamboulelis to consider the idea that there might be a potential to operate faster vessels between Greece and Italy, capable of reducing passage times on the 504-nautical mile route to nearer 20 hours.

Since 1981, Greece had been a member of the European Community and in the intervening period it had enjoyed a period of relative political stability and sustained economic development. By drastically shortening passage times across the Adriatic, it would be possible to bring the country closer to the heart of the European continent and this would be highly advantageous for key national industries such as agriculture and tourism.

Stamboulelis, not being aware that Panagopoulos would soon sell Royal Cruise Line, said nothing of his idea at that time but nonetheless carried out his own private research into the benefits and limitations of a range of fast ro-pax ferry types. In the end, he reasoned that a four-engine conventional ferry with highly optimised hull lines would be the best option as this would enable a large payload of freight to be carried. When Panagopoulos's dream of a new cruise line with large, purpose-built ships appeared to be dashed, Stamboulelis revealed his idea. As he recalls, 'When asked again by our shipbroker, Jean Bernard Raoust, what else could we do, I replied with full confidence "fast ro-pax ferries for short international trade."'

CHAPTER FOUR

THE CREATION OF SUPERFAST

W̶hen Panagopoulos failed to take forward the proposal for catamaran ferries on the Aegean, early in 1992 attention turned instead to Stamboulelis's fast ro-pax idea for large and modern conventional ferries to cross the Adriatic. As Stamboulelis recalls,

'Promoting this new business idea was not easy and although I did eventually obtain Mr. Panagopoulos's consent to look at it, I had to try very hard to make him and his financial executives view the project positively. At that crucial period came the valuable assistance of his son, young Alexander Panagopoulos, who was then doing his military service in the Hellenic Navy, but could still find the time to come to our office for a few hours. Alex quickly embraced the idea and from then on everything proceeded forward quicker and with considerable enthusiasm.'

It was Alexander Panagopoulos who invented the distinctive and highly successful Superfast brand identity. He designed the distinctive funnel shape with upturned wings and strobe lights at the tips and he specified the hull colour – Ferrari red to match the high-speed connotations of the brand. Stamboulelis observes that 'Alex is a ship lover and the design and construction of all Superfast vessels gave him the opportunity to reveal his admirable aesthetic sensibility while being practical at the same time. In terms of design and marketing, he was the driving force of the project.' The brand identity had a unique character which calling the operation 'Panagopoulos Lines' would not have done so effectively.

Pericles Panagopoulos offered Gerasimos Strinzis the possibility of becoming a fifty-fifty partner, but Strintzis declined, preferring to develop further his own ferry business (later, he confessed to regretting this course of action, however). After the decision was made to develop a fast cross-Adriatic ferry business, Attica Enterprises sold all of its non-shipping related activities, leaving only its minority shareholding in Strintzis Lines, while Pericles Panagopoulos retained his private ownership of the Magna Marine

A proud Pericles Panagopoulos at the Schichau Seebeckwerft in 1993 with the keel section of *Superfast I* in the background. *(Costis Stamboulelis collection)*

bulk shipping business.

Attica Enterprises approached several shipyards all over the world to solicit concept designs for fast ro-pax ferries and thereafter started receiving proposals both from European yards and from ones in Japan, none of which fulfilled its requirements. One of the more suitable of the proposals was submitted by the German shipyard Schichau Seebeckwerft of Bremerhaven. It had a considerable reputation for building high-quality roll-on, roll-off vessels; its recent deliveries included examples for TT Line, Olau Line and P&O European Ferries, among others. This was presented to Pericles Panagopoulos who quickly rejected it with barely a second glance, presumably because he felt that it was too utilitarian and lacking any of the sense of style he knew from Royal Cruise Line. Costis Stamboulelis therefore contacted Holger Terpet of Knud E. Hansen

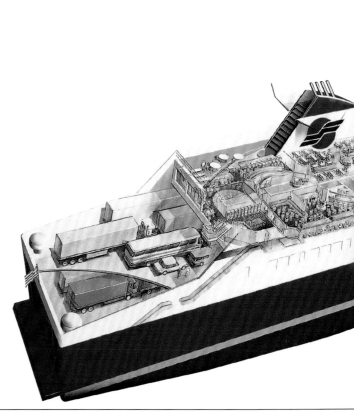

Top: Crucial to the Superfast image was the Ferrari red hull livery and bold graphic identity. *(Bruce Peter)*

Above: Another key feature was the funnel shape, featuring upturned 'winglets' with lasers at their tips to cast patterns of light across the night sky above when in port. *(Bruce Peter)*

Right: A cut-away drawing of the *Superfast I*. *(Attica Group)*

A/S to develop their own design for a large ro-pax ferry capable of achieving a 28-knot maximum speed, using elements of the Schichau Seebeckwerft proposal as its basis. The high-speed was crucial in enabling daily departures from Ancona and Patras with 20-hour direct passages and four hours of turnaround time. Back then, the fastest service provided by competitors was ANEK Lines' 27 hours via Igoumenitsa, using recently-acquired former Japanese vessels. Another well-established competitor, Minoan Lines, was at that time planning on offering 24-hour passages, again via Igoumenitsa, but initially these would not form part of a daily schedule. All the other operators took 33 hours, or more.

To speed up turnarounds, unusually for Greek ferries, the Superfast ships would be drive-through with bow doors; only the freight-orientated operator Ventouris Ferries used this approach on its ro-ro vessels which had originally been built for DFDS North Sea

nearly three-quarters of the internal volume was potentially dedicated to its carriage, the passenger and crew facilities were to be of a high standard, reflecting Pericles Panagopoulos's cruise industry pedigree. A la carte dining, an outdoor swimming pool, a cocktail bar and a nightclub were facilities found on only some Adriatic ferries at that time.

In 1993 an order was placed by Attica Enterprises with Schichau Seebeckwerft for two vessels for Superfast. Their total cost was around 170 million US dollars (or 37 billion drachma). Detailed design work was carried out by the yard with Knud E. Hansen A/S retained to evaluate the drawings.

With regard to the regulations under which the vessels were designed and built, at that time the classification societies were involved in these processes only as far as insuring the application of their own rules were concerned. Verification of satisfying SOLAS, MARPOL and various other national rules mostly concerning passenger and crew accommodation was the responsibility of the Greek Merchant Ship Inspectorate (GMSI). Only with their approval of the plans and of their implementation could a vessel could be registered as a passenger ship under the Greek flag. The Ship Inspectorate is part of the Hellenic Coastguard and headed by Coastguard officers. Shortly after the building contract was signed, Costis Stamboulelis made it a priority to arrange an introductory meeting between representatives of Schichau Seebeckwerft and GMSI at the Hellenic Coastguard's Headquarters. As Stamboulelis recalls,

'All the top brass of the Ship Inspectorate attended and the German shipyard representatives were flattered and delighted. That was a good start and a very cooperative working atmosphere was maintained throughout the construction of the vessels. Regular inspections were carried out by GMSI surveyors – and always with good results.'

Subsequently, similar introductory meetings were convened for all the German, Finnish and South Korean shipyards Attica later placed orders with. Perhaps unsurprisingly, large parts of the eventual design solution were actually quite reminiscent of Schichau Seebeckwerft's other recent ferry projects. Critical for the vessels' success would be their hull form with a pronounced bulb, a slender entry and sleek underwater lines. At the stern, the aft hull lines below the water had a pronounced V-shape with tunnels above the shafts and propellers to give an even wake field and a ducktail sponson to improve efficiency further by slightly increasing the hull's length at

services. All the other Adriatic ferries reversed up to the quays, dropping their anchors to hold position and loading via stern doors only – a slow process and awkward for trucks and coaches, which needed to be carefully driven backwards for stowage.

In terms of layout, the Superfast vessels would use a typical formula for large ro-pax vessels in northern Europe, having three two-deck-high vehicle decks, connected by tilting internal ramps, with passenger and crew accommodation above. The lowest of the vehicle decks was on the tank tops, ahead of the engine room, while the others filled the hull and the lower superstructure, all divided by a centreline casing. The two passenger decks likewise wrapped around this with the public rooms arranged in a U-shape and cabins filling the forward third, forming a distinct 'hotel block' furthest away from the noise of the ventilation and engine uptakes further. Although freight was expected to be the main year-round profit earner and

Shrouded in scaffolding, the superstructure of the **Superfast I** is seen while under construction at Schichau Seebeckwerft in 1994. *(Bruce Peter collection)*

the waterline. The combination had been developed some years before by the MARIN ship research facility at Wageningen in the Netherlands and was known as a 'soft tunnel buttock flow hull form.' Overall, it increased efficiently by 11 per cent and reduced fuel consumption by four per cent. Power was provided by four Sulzer 12-cylinder diesels, generating 34,550 kW. Hull testing was carried out at the Schiffbautechnische Versuchanstalt in Vienna and a considerable amount of Finite Element Methods (FEM) analysis took place to investigate the behaviour of the engine mountings and surrounding steelwork to minimise the possibility of vibrations being transferred through the hull to the passenger accommodation. This approach was at the leading edge of technology and reflected how much further advanced ship design had become since the previous generation of large and fast conventional ferries had been designed in the early-1970s.

The vehicle decks were spacious and remarkably unobstructed, comprising 1,675 lane metres of capacity – a very large amount by the typical standards of Adriatic ferries at that time. In the congested ports of Ancona and Patras, the challenge would be to offload and to get traffic out of the port gates to avoid queues backing up all the way on board. In the wake of a number of ferry accidents caused by flooding of the vehicle decks, followed by sudden loss of stability and rapid capsizing – especially that of the *Estonia* which happened when the hull of the *Superfast I* was already under construction on the slipway – the Superfast vessels were designed beyond the era's regulations with triple bow doors, consisting of a lifting visor, folding vehicle access ramp and a watertight inner folding door, plus a sophisticated closed circuit television monitoring system.

Of the 1,400 passengers carried, 686 would be berthed in *en suite* cabins with the remainder either berthed in couchettes, occupying reclining seats, travelling in deck class or camping aboard inside their mobile homes. This latter method was unique to Adriatic routes and involved plugging these vehicles into the ship's electricity supply, just as one would with a refrigerated lorry trailer. To enable this, the aft section of the upper vehicle deck had large openings in the shell plating to allow fresh air to circulate.

Rather than using a Greek designer to devise interiors as on previous Panagopoulos-owned passenger ships, instead Alexander Panagopoulos decided to use Yran & Storbraaten of Oslo, a firm well-known in the passenger shipping industry for its luxury cruise ship interiors mainly for Norwegian operators, several of which Schichau Seebeckwerft had built in recent years. Unusually for a large ferry, nearly all of the saloons were quite small as opposed to the more typical open-plan layouts favoured for nearly all other ferry

An aerial view of the **Superfast I** while being fitted out at Schichau Seebeckwerft. *(Costis Stamboulelis collection)*

The Ambrosia a la carte restaurant on the **Superfast II**. *(Bruce Peter collection)*

The Calypso Lounge on the **Superfast II**, designed by Yran & Storbraaten. 'Calypso' was a name Panagopoulos had previously used for public rooms on Royal Cruise Line's ships, the primary reference being to Greek mythology - but for many passengers it also conjured up Caribbean dance rhythms. *(Bruce Peter collection)*

The brand new **Superfast I** at Patras; the funnel casing design and livery greatly enhanced what was essentially a quite chunky freight ferry. (*Costis Stamboulelis*)

The cafeteria on the **Superfast II** by Yran & Storbraaten. (*Bruce Peter collection*)

The Aphrodite Lounge on the **Superfast I**. (*Bruce Peter*)

tonnage of the era. Partly, this was due to the central casing necessitating such a layout but was also to a lesser degree an inheritance from Royal Cruise Line whose vessels had a larger number of more intimate spaces than would have been typical of ferries. Nonetheless, with careful planning to consider efficient deployment of shipboard hotel staff, it was possible for passengers to perceive there being a larger than average variety of facilities. There were three bars, including one adjacent to the aft-located swimming pool, a nightclub, three catering outlets comprising an a la carte restaurant, cafeteria and truck driver's restaurant, shops and a casino. While none of these facilities were of a scale or grandeur commensurate with Scandinavian overnight vessels of the era, they were nonetheless outfitted with high-quality materials and they offered a standard of comfort superior to even the newest converted second hand ferries in the Greece-Italy trade. Costis Stamboulelis recalls that 'working with Bjørn Storbraaten was a joyful experience because of his great sense of humour – but it was not always easy because of the cultural differences between Norwegians and Greeks. Even the names we decided to give to the public rooms and their respective signs caused some confusion. We had named one lounge on the *Superfast I* "Calypso" after a nymph in Greek mythology, but the sign produced by Bjorn showed a beautiful girl with a typical Rio carnival outfit dancing calypso.' Alongside a desired aura of comfort and style, the accommodation also needed to be robust, or as Alexander Panagopoulos put it "gorilla-proof" to withstand the very large numbers expected to be transported.

With regard to the latter stages of the vessels' construction, according to Costis Stamboulelis,

'Both Pericles and Alexander Panagopoulos were much involved in the detailed design work as it progressed at Schichau Seebeckwerft and as Bjørn Storbraaten moved on to fine-tune his plans. At the same time, we had Holger Terpet of Knud E. Hansen working with us, assessing our proposals, making corrections to meet regulations and finally incorporating them on drawings which were sent to the shipyard. The expertise of Holger and his attention to the smallest details was of immense value to the shipyard, the interior designers and Attica's newbuilding team alike. Eventually Holger was also employed directly by the yard to assist them in preparing the safety plans of the vessels. Fortunately, as Schichau Seebeckwerft had previously built many large ferries, they were very familiar with processes and materials and they did actually provide us with useful advice regarding installation practices.

'With regard to the design of the officers' and crew's accommodation, there too the Panagopouloses exerted influence. At the time of signing the construction contract with Schichau Seebeckwerft, the Magna Marine Panamax bulk carrier *Panthea* was being dry-docked at the Elefsis Shipyard and so we all went on board for lunch. Pericles Panagopoulos saw the Chinese-type servery rotunda in the officers' mess room and immediately decided that this was how we should organise officer food service on the Superfast vessels. The rotunda solution was therefore adopted and subsequently was specified on all subsequent members of the Superfast fleet.'

In addition to the building of ships, there were many other urgent and challenging tasks to be carried out to bring the Superfast project to fruition. Indeed, the day after the contract to build the *Superfast I* and *Superfast II* was signed, Pericles Panagopoulos told Stamboulelis 'the most urgent matter now is people – we need people.' At that time, the Superfast project consisted of a team of just four or five, including Panagopoulos and his son. The others were Finance Director Charalambos Paschalis, who had been with Panagopoulos since the creation of Royal Cruise Line, John Skoutas, the Technical Manager of Magna Marine whose background before then was in the deep-sea bulk shipping business, and Costis Stamboulelis. The magnitude of the project lying ahead was indeed very big. As Stamboulelis recalls,

'We urgently required to find and employ all kinds of people – those who would staff the supervision team at the shipyard, the officers and key crew members of the ships, the staff of our headquarters to deal with commercial issues and marketing, new port agents in places we had never been before – namely Patras and Ancona – and sales agents in Europe, to name only the most pressing appointments needing made.'

Assembling the supervision team was the first task and, apart from Attica's own key members, it included steel construction experts from Knud E. Hansen A/S and machinery installation specialists from Harpain Shipping, the company owned by Panagopoulos's German broker and good friend, Rimbert Harpain. By the time that the vessels were nearly completed, all the other posts had been filled – an enormous task for which Alexander Panagopoulos was responsible, under the watchful eye and subject to the consent of Panagopoulos Senior. Of key posts, the Financial Directors of

Superfast Ferries and of Attica Holdings, Nicos Tapiris and George Karydis, were both from Royal Cruise Line, as were the Hotel and Customer Services Director, Alexis Economou, the Crew Director, Nicos Kalassarinis, and the Food and Beverage Manager, Costas Sigalas. The Commercial & Marketing Director, Dimitris Andriopoulos, and the Public Relations Director, Yannis Criticos, were however new to Panagopoulos companies.

Attica's newbuilding team supervising the construction of the vessels consisted of Costis Stamboulclis, the naval architect Mike Kardasis, the superintendent engineer Xenofon Plataniotis and Captain Costas Kaintantzis. None of these men had any prior experience of ferry design, Kardasis having previously worked in the oil tanker industry. Stamboulelis had however designed a ferry as a student project while studying at Sunderland Polytechnic and had kept a close eye on ferry design developments in the period since.

As events unfolded, however, it turned out that Superfast would not be having the fast cross-Adriatic ferry market to its self; shortly after Attica Enterprises placed orders for its two Superfast ships with Schichau Seebeckwerft, the ambitious and well-established Cretan-headquartered ferry company Minoan Lines, operating between Patras, Igoumenitsa and Ancona, ordered a new quite fast ferry of its own from Fosen Mekaniske Verksted in Norway. Its 28,417 grt *Aretousa* would, however, be capable of just 23.8 knots – or around three knots slower than Superfast's vessels – and would therefore offer less frequent departures. The other sailings provided by Minoan Lines were operated by older tonnage. On the other hand, the fact that *Aretousa* would stop additionally in Igoumenitsa would enable truckers to embark or disembark there and to drive across Greece, rather than being required to sail all the way to Patras. A lack of calls at Igoumenitsa would prove to be one of the few errors in Superfast's otherwise excellent initial business plan.

Superfast's first ferry, the *Superfast I*, took 18 months to build and, on sea trials early in April 1995, achieved a top speed of 26.85 knots. Apart from the speed being a little less than expected, there was considerable propeller cavitation resulting in noise and vibration in excess of the values specified in the contract. Cavitation is caused by bubbles of air being generated by the shape and rotational movement of propeller blades and it was obvious that the geometry of the existing blade design would have to be slightly changed and so the propeller manufacturer was contacted to offer their professional opinion. Model tests using a revised design of blades were carried out at the Hamburg Schiffbau Versuchanstalt (Hamburg Ship Research Laboratory) and the improved design was from the outset fitted to the second ferry, the *Superfast II*, which additionally had cavitation

observation windows cut into in the bottom of the hull above the propellers in order to verify their performance. Fortunately, the modified blades were successful and the windows were removed and the holes plated over one year later during the ship's guarantee dry-docking.

The bulky exteriors of the two Superfast vessels were given a veneer of sleekness thanks to their bright red and white livery and to the application of dark grey 'go faster' stripes around the windows. Costis Stamboulelis declared himself highly satisfied with the quality of their overall construction and the sophistication of her onboard technologies which were the best yet seen on any Greek ferry. The final hurdle was the issue of the certificates and the registration of the first vessel, always a bureaucratic process which needed good timing and coordination. As Stamboulelis recalls,

'Key staff members of our operational, Crew and Legal departments coordinated the necessary formalities with diverse authorities for the prompt issue of all certificates so that the ship could leave the shipyard under the Greek flag. Copies of the certificates were faxed to the ship while the originals were handed over to a crew member who had been kept back to take them to the ship before it left the Kiel Canal and entered the North Sea on its delivery voyage. No Superfast ferry ever left the building yard certified as a cargo ship thanks to the good coordination of the parties involved and the excellent cooperation of the Greek Merchant Ship Inspectorate.'

In the run-up to the *Superfast I*'s entry into service, Superfast carried out an extensive marketing campaign to create brand awareness and to encourage ticket sales. In an era before websites and online sales, this involved the use of advertising billboards and the distribution of brochures to travel agents' shops throughout Greece, Italy and Germany – the latter being an important source of tourist traffic. Freight hauliers were also targeted to attract them to use the company's fast and qualitatively superior service. The Superfast image was revolutionary and the company's message that its much speedier crossings would enable holidaymakers to enjoy two extra days' holiday was highly effective. Very quickly, Superfast achieved a very high-level of recognition in the minds of the Greek and wider European travelling public. As Attica's Commercial Director, Hercules Simitsidellis, recalls:

'Prior to the launch of Superfast Ferries, Pericles and Alexander Panagopoulos interviewed and recruited professionals from the travel industry to set up their new commercial organisation. A mix of personnel from the airline, cruise, ferry, tour operating, travel and cargo trades, together with flamboyant marketeers formed the nucleus of the new Sales and Marketing Department.

With the announcement of the startup of Superfast Ferries, the challenge was within a short period of time to position and make known to the travel trade, haulers and independent travellers alike the launch of what was to be thought of as the "Ferrari" of the Adriatic Sea, offering a cruise-type quality of services. After many interviews and presentations with top-class advertising agencies, Alexander Panagopoulos with his marketing team engaged an international advertising company to prepare Superfast Ferries communication plan and advertising campaign.

The company invested heavily with advertisements in the international media, participated in trade and consumer exhibitions in Europe, created merchandise and brochures, launched a loyalty programme called "Seasmiles" for haulers and passengers, designed fashionable staff uniforms for crew and staff at shore, constructed port and sales offices in the same house style making use of Superfast/Ferrari red and set up billboards on all major highways leading to the ports. Within a short period of time the brand "Superfast Ferries" was very well-known across Europe.

Sales calls at the premises of potential freight customers and participation at trade and consumer exhibitions led to agreements with haulers, cargo companies, tour operators, travel agents, ethnic community travel specialists, incentive houses. All of this was achieved within only a short period of time and was a considerable achievement by all involved.

In Ancona and Patras, experienced port agents were engaged to communicate with the relevant authorities, suppliers and service providers to set up the operational and servicing solutions for the new vessels. Superfast Ferries with its state-of-the-art, luxurious high-speed vessels, offering a reliable, a punctual and friendly service managed within a short period of time, to position itself as the first choice among trade and travelers.'

So far as crewing was concerned, Royal Cruise Line was found to be a very good resource for experienced shipboard staff, especially cabin and restaurant stewards who were easily lured away to work again with their old boss, Pericles Panagopoulos, on Greek-owned ships operating much closer to home than RCL's American-based and, by then, Bahamian-flagged cruise vessels. As Stamboulelis observes,

'The employment of people coming from the cruise industry and used to serving American passengers had a tremendous positive impact on the service standard on board. Tourists and especially truck drivers had not experienced such VIP treatment before during their Adriatic voyages, nor were they used to the pristine condition in which the Superfast ships were maintained. The cruise ship standard was greatly appreciated.'

On 15 April, the *Superfast I* entered service between Patras and Ancona with the *Superfast II* following on 11 June, enabling Superfast to provide a two-ship service with daily departures in each direction. Yet, as Costis Stamboulelis recalls, at first, the Superfast operation experienced some teething problems:

'The success of the whole concept depended heavily on an efficient port operation and a quick unloading and loading of the vessels. The turnaround time had to be as short as possible. Already during the construction of the vessels, Pericles Panagopoulos had expressed his concern about this and had asked our captains to study their garage and ramp layout and produce loading plans or make recommendations for changes. The first call of *Superfast I* in the port of Patras was a nightmarish experience because the pier was too low compared with the main deck of the vessel and the stern ramps could not be inclined by more than seven degrees. We witnessed trucks practically jumping off the ship. It was the same situation in the port of Ancona.

Captain Molfesis, our agent, Renato Morandi, and I went during the night to an overgrown junk yard to search for some old steel ramps ANEK Lines had once used in the port and which were abandoned there. The old steel ramps were found and although they were not quite high enough they did help until our own steel ramps were manufactured in Greece and transported in sections by Superfast and positioned and secured on the pier where they still stand today. In a similar way, concrete ramps were constructed in the port of Patras. Unfortunately, the port authorities of both Patras and Ancona did not help in improving the shore infrastructure. Shortly after the orders for the *Superfast I* and *Superfast II* had been placed, Attica had asked the ships' access equipment maker,

The *Superfast I* is seen arriving at Patras with spectators in the foreground. In those days, unlike today, the quays of Mediterranean ports were open to the public and so ships with a strong visual image could attract positive attention. *(Bruce Peter)*

MacGregor, to design an appropriate link span for unloading the vessels' upper decks directly ashore. Full studies were carried out – including anti-seismic calculations – and when the proposal was ready, Attica informed the port authorities that they were willing to pay for all the necessary work and effectively donate the structures to them. Strange as it may seem, Attica's very generous offer was not accepted.'

Without double-level linkspans, or even the ability to unload and load via the bow door, drive-through operations were impossible and so the *Superfast I* and *Superfast II* needed to berth stern-in and only use their rear ramps for all access, including that of passengers. The lengthened port turnarounds highlighted the vessels' slightly slower than expected speed and so, rather than maintaining the same arrival and departure times on a daily basis, as had been the initial intention, it was necessary instead to stagger these with later arrivals and departures on each day of the week. Nonetheless, their manoeuvrability in port could not be faulted, as Stamboulelis further recalls:

'Apart from controllable pitch propellers and bow thrusters, the vessels were fitted with Becker flap rudders which gave them capabilities virtually unknown in Greece until then. Greek captains – especially those of ferries and cruise ships – are renowned for their skill in manoeuvring their vessels in very difficult circumstances, caused by cramped ports with inadequate shore infrastructure often combined with adverse weather conditions. Much as we liked the manoeuvrability aspect of the flap rudders, we decided not to specify them in our next vessels because they had been blamed for contributing to the cavitation we had experienced during the sea trials. According to subsequent investigations by the manufacturer, the main problem was the thick leading edge of the rudder.'

The bridge equipment was state-of-the-art and a novelty for Greek ferries was the fitment of 'joysticks' on consoles in the bridge wings to manoeuvre the vessels with fingertip accuracy. When the *Superfast I* arrived at Patras, the system supplier, KaMeWa, gave the officers of both ships a demonstration of their use and capabilities during a short circuit of the sea outside the harbour. In service, however, the captains never used the joysticks, preferring traditional methods of control with which they were already familiar. Nonetheless, the feature continued to be specified for all subsequent Superfast ships because it was thought that it would add to their resale value.

Costis Stamboulelis and his wife, Eleni, were travelling on the *Superfast I*'s second northbound voyage from Patras to Ancona when, during the early hours of the morning, they realised that the vessel was not moving and, looking out of their cabin window, they could see a frigate about one mile distant. As Stamboulelis recalls,

'I telephoned the bridge and was informed by Captain Molfesis that a frigate of the Turkish Navy – a member of the NATO fleet enforcing the arms embargo against Yugoslavia – was on duty on that particular day in the Strait of Otranto. The *Superfast I* had been ordered to stop for inspection and, shortly afterwards, a team of navy commandos came in a rubber boat and boarded the vessel. They inspected the bridge and the garages and asked the Captain about the ship, its cargo and destination. When they were satisfied they returned back to their frigate and allowed us to continue our voyage. Their excuse was that nobody had informed NATO command that a new fast ferry would be trading between Greece and Italy and the Turkish commander thought that a strange, unknown and fast ship was trying to break the blockade. After the incident our agents did inform all authorities accordingly and we continued trading unobstructed from then on.'

Superfast's operation had a profound impact on the subsequent development of the Adriatic ferry market. Both freight and passenger loadings were greater than had been forecast and, particularly out with the summer season, the higher numbers of passengers carried was very gratifying. Pericles Panagopoulos was very pleased, telling Stamboulelis, 'we have to congratulate ourselves because, newcomers as we were in this ferry market, we made very few mistakes'. According to Costis Stamboulelis:

'The first year of operation was a test period in which the Superfast concept met with tremendous success both with regard to passenger satisfaction and the support of trucking and freight logistics companies. The service set new standards which were subsequently widely adopted by other ferry companies in Greece and elsewhere. Pericles and Alexander Panagopoulos were fully convinced that their boldness was well founded.'

Less than a month after the *Superfast I* entered service, however,

Superfast's well-established rival, Minoan Lines, soon began to copy its style by adding the words 'High Speed' to the hulls of its newest and fastest ferries, such as the **Pasiphae Palace**, seen here in 2000 leaving Patras with the **Erotokritos** in the foreground. *(Bruce Peter)*

Minoan Lines introduced the *Aretousa* which although a slower vessel was conceptually broadly similar to Superfast's units, though lacking their novel visual identity (Eventually, Minoan Lines' had 'High-Speed' painted in large red letters on her hull topsides in an attempt to emulate Superfast's graphic approach). As events unfolded, the three ferries were merely the first of a large armada of new tonnage for the Greece to Italy routes. Within less than a decade, Superfast and Minoan Lines had each commissioned at least ten new large and fast ro-pax vessels and, in addition, Strintzis Lines and ANEK Lines also ordered new tonnage for their prime Adriatic routes. From being a ferry market characterised primarily by ageing vessels, the Greece-Italy trade suddenly became host to many of the newest and most advanced ferries in the world. The smaller operators who could not have afforded such largesse thereafter struggled and several withdrew altogether.

Minoan Lines' subsequent new ferries, the 30,010 grt *Ikarus* and *Pasiphae*, delivered from Fosen in Norway in 1997 and 1998 respectively, were 26.4-knot vessels, better able to maintain closer parity with Superfast's in terms of typical voyage durations. All of the subsequent deliveries to Minoan, Strintzis and ANEK were capable of speeds in the 27-30 knot range. In other words, the *Superfast I* and *Superfast II* set the paradigm against which a whole generation of Adriatic ferries were designed and operated.

CHAPTER FIVE

SUPERFAST'S ERA OF EXPANSION

Around a year after the *Superfast I* and *Superfast II* entered service, Pericles and Alexander Panagopoulos decided to order the second pair of ferries of an enhanced design – the *Superfast III* and *Superfast IV*. With no possibility of getting access to better port infrastructure any time soon, Superfast specified a higher service speed for these ships. The plan was that they would replace the *Superfast I* and *Superfast II* between Patras and Ancona and that these vessels would then inaugurate a new route between Patras, Igoumenitsa and Bari, a major ferry port further south on Italy's Adriatic coast, from which the voyage duration to Greece was somewhat shorter and with slightly less passenger traffic than from Ancona.

The approach to project development commenced with the *Superfast I* and *Superfast II* became standard practice for the procurement of all subsequent Superfast vessels, as Costis Stamboulelis records:

'In every Attica newbuilding project, we began by generating a preliminary general arrangement plan and specification in cooperation with our consultants, Knud E. Hansen A/S, and with our interior designers for the passenger accommodation. These would be presented to the shipyards and the one selected would make its own comments on the GA plan, mainly with regard to the hull form, structural modifications such as the position of pillars and bulkheads and provide its input for machinery spaces, tank arrangements, escape routes, cable and pipe trunks and various other service spaces. Once developed in this manner to the satisfaction of all concerned, the shipyard's own more detailed version of the GA plan would be attached to the build contract.

The specification – which was the other attachment to the contract – was also negotiated with the shipyard and all details were agreed between the parties. The process varied from yard to yard. Some shipyards had too many items they wanted to revise while others were prepared to accept our proposals with only minor changes. The specification is a very important document, practically every word of which carries a price tag. Shipyards want to make certain that their scope of supply is very clearly defined and reflected in their quotation. The ship owner, on the other hand, wants to make certain that all their requirements are included in the shipyard's scope of supply so that as far as possible nothing can be claimed later as an extra cost. Apart from costs of materials, equipment and installation, shipyards are always concerned about costs for meeting specified requirements for speed, deadweight capacity and comfort levels among others and, much worse from their point of view, penalty costs for failing to meet such requirements.'

As the new vessels would be too big for Schichau Seebeckwerft's slipway, another potential German builder was Howaldtswerke Deutsche Werft in Kiel, where the Managing Director, Dr. Jürgen Gollenbeck, was an old acquaintance of Pericles Panagopoulos from Royal Cruise Line days – but unfortunately their bid was too expensive.

The shipyard which successfully tendered to build the 29,067gt *Superfast III* and *Superfast IV* was Kværner Masa-Yards in Turku in Finland. As with Schichau Seebeckwerft, Kværner Masa-Yards was a highly experienced ferry builder which had constructed many of the largest and most innovative Baltic cruise ferries of the 1980s. Since that time, new orders had been harder to find and so the yard accepted whatever ferry building work it could get – most recently, a comparatively basic ro-pax vessel for Trasmediterranea in Spain, the *Juan J. Sister*, which was completed in 1993 with the benefit of a state subvention. To win the Superfast orders from Attica Enterprises, further subventions were received, meaning that vessels of considerably higher specification than the *Superfast I* and *Superfast II*

The *Superfast III* is seen under construction at Kværner Masa-Yards Turku shipyard in late-1997. *(Meyer Turku)*

The *Superfast III* in the building dock at Kværner Masa-Yards in Turku. *(Meyer Turku)*

The *Superfast IV* is seen when nearly completed at the outfitting quay in Turku early in 1998. *(Krystof Brzoza)*

Top: The **Superfast III** in the Kiel Canal in evening light during its delivery voyage from Turku to Greece in February 1998. (*Marko Stampehl*)

Above: The main lounge on the **Superfast III,** designed by Apostolos Molindris in a more sleeker style than the equivalent spaces on the first two Superfasts. (*Bruce Peter*)

Right: A stern-quarter view of the **Superfast III** in the Kiel Canal during its delivery voyage. (*Marko Stampehl*)

could be built at the relatively moderate cost of approximately 100 million US dollars each. As the design for the first pair belonged to Schichau Seebeckwerft and as Kværner Masa-Yards in any case had its own favoured approaches for ferry design and detailing, it produced an entirely new solution, albeit following the same basic layout formula as for the initial vessels. Only the funnel shape and the livery were exactly the same as before. In addition to the keenly-priced bid by Kværner Masa-Yards, the shipyard was also made attractive by the fact it had previously produced designs for even faster ro-pax ferries as a part of a publicly-funded innovative ship development project called 'Telakka 2000', and the experiences gained from these were undoubtedly useful when designing the Superfast pair in detail.

Kværner Masa-Yards' founder and CEO was Martin Saarikangas – a highly experienced shipbuilder and also an almost cult figure in Finnish public life. Physically very large and with a personality to match, he had worked in the industry since the 1950s.

spoke. All the others who had daily contact with us kept completely silent and I was quite impressed by how well informed Saarikangas was'.

The Finnish naval architecture consultancy Deltamarin, which had a peripheral role in the development of the first two Superfasts, was employed to assist in designing in detail and managing the construction of the new vessels. Particular attention was paid to the hull design and manoeuvrability while the service speed was increased to enable slightly faster crossings and the same daily schedule. Consequently, more powerful 16-cylinder Wärtsilä-Sulzer diesels were installed than on the initial pair. Initially Kværner Masa-Yards offered a new type of engine designed in Vaasa but built by Wärtsilä's recently-acquired Dutch subsidiary, Stork Werkspoor. However, as Pericles Panagopoulos had previously had bad experiences with Stork Werkspoor engines, he insisted that Sulzer units be used instead.

With the exception of Captain Kaintantzis who had stayed behind to take care of the Superfast Operation, Attica's supervisory team consisted of the same individuals as had worked with Schichau Seebeckwerft, though with an additional naval architect, John Revelas, and the electrical and electronics expert, Myron Vergis. Attica wanted to avoid the noise and vibration problems experienced on *Superfast I* and *Superfast II* and so in cooperation with Knud E. Hansen A/S they added strict noise and vibration limits into the specification for the new vessels. Kværner Masa-Yards – which in any case already had a good reputation for building quiet passenger ships – went to a great deal of trouble to ensure that the structural design and the selection of certain machinery would ensure that these limits would not be exceeded. One of these steps was their recommendation of Schelde reduction gears, which were known to be the quieter of the various gear systems available at that time. Attica's engineers were at first hesitant because the type was unfamiliar to them, but nonetheless they acceded to the yard's strong insistence. Careful attention to insulation, to the correct mounting of all the machinery and to the alleviation of vibration resonance wherever it occurred meant that even when operating at 30 knots, the impression in the passenger and crew accommodation was of being stationary.

Whereas the superstructures of the initial West German-built Superfasts were rather rectilinear with a close aesthetic affinity with freighter tonnage, the Finnish-built ones had slanted and curved forward aspects, more resembling those of recent Turku-built Baltic cruise ferries. Another important change was the specification of

More recently, in the late-1980s he had rescued and re-structured the company after the bankruptcy of its previous owner, Wärtsilä Marine (and thereby saved a large part of the Finnish shipbuilding industry). It was Saarikangas who negotiated Kværner Masa-Yards' offer with Pericles Panagopoulos. As Costis Stamboulelis recalls,

'When I arrived at the Yard in Turku, I sensed immediately the high respect Mr Saarikangas commanded – next only to the almighty God, although for a lot of the Finns I subsequently worked alongside, Saarikangas actually was God. He resided normally in Helsinki, but visited Turku regularly especially whenever he was informed of disputes between Attica and the yard. In one such case Alexander Panagopoulos and I were invited to dinner at his summer residence together with between 12 and 15 engineers from the yard. After eating and drinking, the discussion about problems in the building progress was opened and it was only Mr Saarikangas who

The 'Les Amis' a la carte restaurant on the **Superfast III**. *(Bruce Peter)*

Part of the newly-completed hallway and the shop (with the shelves not yet stocked) on the **Superfast III**. *(Meyer Turku)*

clam shell-type bow doors, which opened outwards and back to the sides, instead of a lifting visor as on the earlier vessels. Costis Stamboulelis recalls that 'the opening and closing of the 45-ton visor of the *Superfast I* and *Superfast II* was a scary operation that I did not like. We only ever used it three or four times, but that was enough for me.'

Inboard, more consideration was given to a cruise-style passenger environment with a larger number of cabin berths (810 versus 686 on the initial pair) and a lido area, surrounded by protective glass screens, between the mast and funnel where the earlier vessels had a set of rather utilitarian ventilators protruding from the top of the centreline casing. Although the final design was produced in Finland, Knud E. Hansen A/S was retained to evaluate the plans on behalf of the owner and to suggest improvements (this work was again carried out by Holger Terpet).

The interiors of the *Superfast III* and *Superfast IV* were designed by a young Athens-based architect, Apostolos Molindris, who for the previous ten years had been an employee of AMK, the design firm owned by Michalis Katzourakis and his wife, Agni, which in the past had produced artworks and interiors for Royal Cruise Line's vessels. Molindris had studied architecture at the University of Thessaloniki, working thereafter in the firms of Tzonos and Hoipel & Hoipel before joining AMK. When in 1996 Katzourakis was approached by Pericles and Alexander Panagopoulos to request that he take on the commission to produce interiors for the vessels, he was at first hesitant as, although he was well-known for cruise ship interiors, he had never previously worked on any ro-pax ferries. It was in fact Molindris who persuaded him and who ultimately became responsible for the design work. At the same time Yran and Storbraaten were invited to submit a proposal and, subsequently, the submissions were presented one after the other by the two firms of architects at a high-level meeting attended by Pericles and Alexander Panagopoulos and Costis Stamboulelis and by a five-person team from Kværner Masa. The Panagopouloses chose the design by Michalis Katzourakis's firm, which Molindris presented. In particular, Alexander Panagopoulos and Molindris found that they

The mast of the ***Superfast III*** with wings matching those on the funnel casing. *(Bruce Peter)*

got on well at a personal level and they were also about the same age. As he observes, 'I was extremely fortunate to get to know Pericles and Alexander Panagopoulos. If Alexander hadn't introduced himself as a client, I would have thought of him as a colleague. We very quickly had a rapport and he contributed to the design process his very sharp perception of space, colour and texture, as well as valuable business insight.' Molindris's approach appeared warmer and more slickly up-to-date than Yran & Storbraaten's interiors for the earlier ships had been. In particular, he made inventive use of ceiling finishes and lighting to lend distinctive atmospheres to the public rooms and passageways. In the stairways, saturated colours and bold number graphics identified each deck to aid orientation.

Molindris had already established his own design consultancy, Molindris + Associates, while continuing to work with Katzourakis and he was keen to find his own clients. Besides, he already had expertise in working with other ship owners, having recently designed the interiors of the Chandris shipping company's headquarters in Piraeus. Shortly after the *Superfast III* and *Superfast IV* commissions

were awarded to him, he was invited by Alexander Panagopoulos also to design a new headquarters for Attica, which was located in the Athens district of Voula. Thereafter, Molindris + Associates were commissioned to produce the interiors for all of the subsequent Superfast vessels.

Meanwhile, construction of the *Superfast III* and *Superfast IV* commenced in Turku. As Costis Stamboulelis recalls, although these projects generally progressed very smoothly, there were occasional fundamental issues of disagreement between Attica's team and the shipyard's management:

'I once had a strong confrontation with Martin Saarikangas when apart from concerns about extra costs there were worries about the first vessel's increasing weight. Our problems actually began shortly after the contract had been signed. The classification society we had selected was the American Bureau of Shipping and the yard had accepted this but, before signing the contract, they had already calculated the steel weight of the vessels according to the rules of a different classification society, Lloyd's Register of Shipping, and it apparently did not occur to them that there could be differences between the methods employed by the two classification societies. They soon found out that applying the rules of American Bureau of Shipping would result in a heavier steel construction and they got alarmed when seeing that their own margin was rapidly consumed not by additional requirements from our side but only by applying ABS's rules.

At a certain point when the disagreement between Attica Enterprises and the yard about extra costs had multiplied, Martin Saarikangas communicated with Pericles Panagopoulos and a meeting was arranged in Turku. Meanwhile, Alexander Panagopoulos and I had prepared our figures and arguments regarding costs but the discussion got a bit intense when he associated the extra costs problem with the extra weight one. Martin Saarikangas said to me "As a naval architect you should know what weight distribution means to the stability of a vessel" to which I replied "I do know what it means, but I do not know the results of your calculations about which you have not informed us, so in fact I do not know where we stand at this moment". "We are at the limit" he said.

It was then when Pericles Panagopoulos took Martin into another room leaving Alexander, me and the rest of us Fins and Greeks waiting at the table. A short while afterwards, the

The *Superfast III* is seen alongside at Patras; in comparison with the *Superfast I*, illustrated on page 26, it will be seen that the design details are considerably more refined and harmonious. *(Bruce Peter)*

two gentlemen walked out of the room looking pleased and relaxed. The matter of the extra costs had been settled. When a few days later I complained to Mr. P. that he had not given us the chance to present our case, he told me that Saarikangas and I had looked like cocks ready to fight and he had to stop it.'

For the Greek supervisory team, another major challenge was the cold Finnish climate, which southern Europeans found very uncomfortable:

'The initial visit in winter of Alexander Panagopoulos, the interior architect Apostolos Molindris and myself to Kværner Masa-Yards' Piikio works, where ships' cabins were prefabricated, for the inspection of mock up cabins was fortunately brief, but the permanent stay in Turku for 13 months during the construction and outfitting period was a hard test for Attica's permanent project team. I personally had also the bad feeling of being isolated from the rest of Europe, especially after the evening departures of cruise ferries to Stockholm. Fortunately, progress on the construction of the vessels was interrupted in the building dock only two or three times during the 1997 winter because of extremely low temperatures which meant that even the Finns had to down tools and retreat indoors.'

The sea trials of the two vessels were completed successfully, although those of *Superfast III* took longer than had been anticipated because of repeated breakdowns of various pieces of machinery and equipment. It was necessary for the yard to borrow a tug to shuttle several times to the ship to bring out replacement parts or pieces of equipment removed from *Superfast IV*, which the Attica supervisory team eventually started referring to as 'the spare ship'.

When these challenges were resolved, the vessels departed on their delivery voyages, *Superfast III* entering service between Patras and Ancona in February 1998 and the *Superfast IV* – on the delivery voyage of which Pericles and Alexander Panagopoulos travelled – commencing operation two months thereafter in April. With these developments, Superfast now could offer two daily Adriatic routes using four ports of call – Patras and Igoumenitsa in Greece and Ancona and Bari in Italy. The departures from Italy were scheduled in the early and late evening so that trucks coming from the country's industrial north had enough time to get to the ports for embarkation. The Panagopouloses were extremely pleased with the vessels, as a speech by Alexander Panagopoulos, made at the delivery of the *Superfast III*, demonstrates: 'For the first time I can honestly say that all our expectations have been surpassed… We are getting ships that are faster, larger, more economic and more comfortable than we expected.'

Both Pericles and Alexander Panagopulos kept close scrutiny over Superfast's day-to-day operations. When some minor infelicity attracted their attention they would politely but firmly communicate with the relevant personnel to have it corrected. As Hercules Simitsidellis recalls,

'On my first working day at Attica Group, I received a call asking what time our vessel from Bari would be arriving at Patras. I responded "I think the vessel arrives at 12.30 local time". The response was "in our company we don't think, we know". From that date onwards, I made sure "we knew" in case I was ever asked again. On another occasion when I was visiting one of our vessels at the port of Igoumenitsa late in the evening, I was informed that out of the blue Mr Panagopoulos had appeared. He embarked the vessel on his own and made his way through all public spaces, cabins, bridge and engine room, closely examining everything as he went. When he encountered me he remarked "I see we have a restaurani on this vessel". We did not understand his remark immediately, but later saw that the "t" in the word restaurant on the sign outside its entrance had been smeared with brass cleaner. On a later date, Mr. Panagopoulos was travelling from Patras to Ancona and, whilst sitting in the aft lounge, he spotted a spelling mistake in the terms and conditions on the cover of a ticket. Alarm was signalled in all directions and the fault was corrected on all new tickets issued before his return trip two days later. Such findings electrified the whole organisation and ensured that the staff were alert and pro-active in trying to be accurate in the information we produced and precise in the details of service provision. This resulted in operational excellence, earning Superfast widespread reputations as a leading high-quality ferry operator.'

Superfast's Adriatic operations were such a great success that Alexander Panagopulos, who had by then become an increasingly

The ***Superfast III*** approaches Patras with Minoan Lines' ***Erotokritos*** in the foreground at Easter 2001. *(Bruce Peter)*

dominant force in Attica Enterprises, decided that Superfast should be expanded with new routes and that Attica Enterprises should order a further four ferries for delivery between 1998 and 2001 to operate on these. According to Costis Stamboulelis,

'Even before the *Superfast III* and *Superfast IV* had been completed, the news was already out that Attica was going to order more vessels and so shipyards wanted to know what size and layout we had in mind. The Italian shipbuilder, Fincantieri, which was one major European yard with which we regularly held talks with but never concluded in a contract, sent incognito a four or five-person delegation to meet me in Turku to discuss our next project. Our meeting was held during evening hours in their hotel and they left the next morning to prepare an offer for us. As previously, they were too expensive but nonetheless their top salesman told me he did not mind spending time talking with Attica as long as he was signing contracts with other companies at the same time.'

Another keen contender for the rumoured new Attica contracts was Howaldtswerke Deutsche Werft in Kiel. Indeed, its Chairman,

Dr. Jürgen Gollenbeck, and senior management were so keen to win orders that when the *Superfast IV* was *en route* from Turku to Patras via the Kiel Canal with Pericles and Alexander Panagopoulos on board, they visited the ship, bringing along their naval architects to begin negotiations and to study the type of specifications, fit and finish that Attica would be requiring.

Attica's plan was to order four vessels for delivery in 2001, all of which were at first intended for operation on Mediterranean routes. The first two were for service between Patras and Ancona with a call at Igoumenitsa on the way and the second pair were initially intended to inaugurate an entirely new Superfast service between Ancona in Italy and Çesme on the west coast of Turkey. At that time, there were many elderly ferries plodding slowly between Greece and Turkey carrying trucks all-year-round and holidaymakers during the summer. A Superfast service appeared likely to achieve a similar transformation to the Italy-Turkey ferry trade as had been realised

Top: The **Superfast VI** nears completion at Howaldtswerke Deutsche Werft in Kiel in the autumn of 2000. *(Bruce Peter)*

Left: An aerial view of the quays at Patras showing, top to bottom, the **Superfast IV**, **Superfast VI**, **Superfast III** and **Superfast I**. *(Attica Group)*

between Italy and Greece. Unfortunately, between the Panagopouloses having this idea – which was first considered in 1998 – and an order being agreed, in the spring of 1999, political relations between Turkey and Greece soured as a result of a number of minor naval skirmishes in disputed territory off the Turkish coast. This suddenly unpropitious context caused Pericles and Alexander Panagopoulos to change their plans radically and instead to consider using the two vessels earmarked for the Turkey service in an entirely new market for a Greek ferry owner – the Baltic Sea. That this might be a possibility had first been planted in their minds some years previously by a Danish travel industry and shipping entrepreneur, Rudolf Bier, whom Pericles Panagopoulos had first met in the early-1970s when the Royal Cruise Line ship *Golden Odyssey* was being built in Denmark at the Helsingør Shipyard. At that time, Bier was briefly serving as the managing director of the Danish ferry and liner shipping company, DFDS, which owned the yard. A little earlier, in 1971, Bier had taken the bold step of redeploying a pair of redundant DFDS Danish domestic ferries of recent construction on routes across the western and eastern Mediterranean; these were the *Dana Sirena* and *Dana Corona*, which introduced one-class, cruise-style services with entertainment in a market at that time dominated by ferry operators offering only much more utilitarian transportation. A quarter-of-a-century later the entrepreneurial Bier sought to persuade Pericles Panagopoulos that it would be a good idea to bring his Superfast concept to the Baltic Sea with a triangular fast ro-pax route linking Finland, eastern Sweden and Germany's Baltic coast. As Costis Stamboulelis recollects,

'Mr Bier's proposal was discussed extensively in Greece and in Denmark, but for the time being it was put aside. When the Panagopouloses decided that it would be unwise to pursue the Italy-Turkey project, new routes would have to be found for at least two of the vessels that Attica were ready to order and it was then that Mr Bier's Baltic project was brought back on the table.'

Whereas Bier's plan had envisaged fast ferries in constant circulation between the three countries, the Panagopouloses decided that a point-to-point service would be better and that a seemingly obvious route on which speed would be advantageous was between the south-western tip of Finland and the German Baltic coast as there was no alternative for trucks than sea travel. Since 1977, Finland had been linked by sea with the then-West Germany by the pioneering gas turbine-powered high-speed cruise-ferry *Finnjet* which

operated between Helsinki and Travemünde, completing each passage in 22 hours. The vessel guzzled expensive jet fuel and the route was only viable due to the Cold War 'Iron Curtain' which cut off ports in Eastern Europe that were much closer to Finland. Finnlines also provided a slower freight-orientated service, taking around 30 hours. What Superfast would be providing in addition would be a hybrid of the two, combining *Finnjet*-style speed and comfort with Finnlines' ability to carry freight. Besides, the Finnjet was ageing and much progress had been made since with regard to the propulsion efficiency and hydrodynamic design of fast conventional ferries.

When preparing for the new Baltic Superfast route, Attica's management first contacted the management of the port of Rostock in the former German Democratic Republic which they believed would be the ideal location for Superfast's continental hub, giving easy access to the heart of Europe. Attica's managers visited Rostock to discuss the port's potential and were warmly welcomed by the city's mayor and by Dr. Ulrich Bauermeister, the port's Managing Director, both of whom agreed to provide the best possible assistance and support. Next, they contacted the port manager in Helsinki who, as Costis Stamboulelis recalls,

'…Gave us a frosty reception when we visited him which was a good match for the prevailing winter weather conditions. We are told that it would be impossible for us to use either of the three main ferry ports in the city centre but that we might at some unspecified point in the future be allowed access to a planned new freight port at Vuosaari, some way to the east of Helsinki.'

The long distance from Vuosaari to Rostock, combined with the fact that when built it would not be suitable for passengers, led Attica to decide to find another port closer to Germany. Hanko was then proposed and as Attica's managers were running short of time, they chartered a helicopter to take them there and straight back to Helsinki airport in time for their flight to Germany. As Costis Stamboulelis recalls,

'My first visit to Hanko had been back in 1997 during the construction of *Superfast III* and *Superfast IV* in Turku. I visited it out of curiosity and recall driving on a road heading south along a small and rather desolate peninsula, at the end of which was a very small and isolated port where a Transfennica

The impressive-looking **Superfast V** at speed on the Adriatic between Patras and Igoumenitsa. *(Bruce Peter)*

Part of the circulation space in the **Superfast V**'s passenger accommodation with panels comprising patterned glass tiles forming an image of a seascape. *(Apostolos Molindris)*

One of the colour-coded stairways in the **Superfast V**. *(Apostolos Molindris)*

ro-ro freight vessel was loading. At that time, I could not have imagined that four years later this same port would become Superfast's main gateway to Finland. The reception we were given in Hanko was much warmer than the one we had received in Helsinki and we soon found a way to build a link span and a long passenger embarkation bridge in spite of the fact that the port did not have anything like as big a managerial organisation as in Helsinki or Rostock.'

With regard to the construction of the first of the new series of Superfast vessels at Howldtswerke Deutsche Werft, Costis Stamboulelis remembers:

'When we first visited the shipyard, we could immediately appreciate its big production capacity, but at the same time we could see that it had seen better days. The huge graving dock was empty and other than some naval submarine construction there was no sign of any other activity. A number of buildings had been abandoned and left without any repair or maintenance, which gave us the opportunity to choose the best location we ever had in any yard for our supervision office - right in the centre of all activities between the graving dock and the outfitting pier. The management of the yard quickly had the part of the building we were to occupy refurbished and we moved in for a stay that would last for nearly three years. We were aware that HDW did not have any recent experience in designing big ro-pax ferries, but were somehow comforted by the presence of a few people we knew from their work in other yards in the past – the most important of whom was the Chairman, Dr. Jürgen Gollenbeck.'

As with Attica's ferry projects in Finland, initial designs for the ferries ordered from Howaldtswerke Deutsche Werft were produced by Holger Terpet of Knud E. Hansen A/S working in close collaboration with Costis Stamboulelis and his colleagues. HDW's own naval architects then produced their own more detailed versions, which Terpet helped to evaluate and modify as necessary. Given the size of the order, the existing Attica newbuilding team from the Finnish projects was strengthened by the addition of three extra naval architects – George Anagnostou, Chris-Alexander Korfiatis and John Speis. Apart from an aft lounge with the two-deck-high window wall the *Superfast V* and *Superfast VI* were to be similar in layout to the *Superfast III* and *Superfast IV*, though with a slightly higher service speed of 29 knots to enable enough time for a call at

Igoumenitsa while *en route* between Patras and Ancona (whereas the existing vessels sailed non-stop between the two end ports). As Costis Stamboulelis recounts,

'The detailed designs for the *Superfast V* and *Superfast VI* were still being worked out when the design office of the yard contacted us to let us know that they were having some difficulties in implementing the specification. At a certain point

The *Superfast V*'s aft-facing lounge. *(Bruce Peter)*

the yard's management thought they should invite Mr. Panagopoulos over to explain the problems – and so they did. At a meeting over dinner, the yard's people opened several plans in front of us and started explaining where they were having difficulties. This took a considerable time and appeared to be leading nowhere useful. In the end, I had to tell them that we simply wanted another *Superfast III*, only 10 metres longer, to which Mr. Panagopoulos agreed fully. Then we suggested that it would be a good idea if HDW were to contact Kværner Masa-Yards to see if they could get some of the production plans of the *Superfast III*. These, we felt, would greatly assist them and eventually they did purchase some plans, but I don't know which ones exactly.'

HDW's traditionalist approach came as a surprise to Attica's supervisory team, who had become used to the advanced methods

A section of the cafeteria on the **Superfast V**. *(Apostolos Molindris)*   The **Superfast V**'s a la carte restaurant. *(Apostolos Molindris)*

used to design the ferries built in Finland:

> 'As with every other project, the yard had to use the specification and GA plan we had provided as a basis for designing the engine room arrangement. To do so, they produced a vast timber and Perspex model of the space and all of its equipment and pipework which we were asked to review. Making such a model was certainly an old-fashioned method in the days of 3-D Computer Aided Design, but it was nonetheless very impressive and gave our engineers the possibility of assessing it from every angle, including checking access to all of the equipment for easy maintenance and the replacement of bulky machinery parts.'

With regard to smooth sailing and control of vibration, HDW was keen to emulate or improve upon the high standards achieved on the Finnish-built Superfast vessels. Indeed, according to Costis Stamboulelis,

> 'The yard was so anxious to avoid vibrations of any kind that they overdesigned all of the foundations and supports not only in the engine room but also in the public areas and open decks too. Upon seeing the massive foundation of the two-deck high window wall in the aft lounges, I wondered if it was really

necessary. Another cause of extra weight was the insufficient coordination of plans to find the optimum routes for cables and pipes in order to reduce their quantity and length with the consequence that the *Superfast V* was somewhat heavier than had been calculated. Fortunately, the yard identified the mistakes made which were not repeated on the subsequent vessels.'

The difficulties in designing and building the *Superfast V* and *Superfast VI* were exacerbated by turmoil in HDW's senior management. In February 1999 the yard's experienced chairman, Dr Jürgen Gollenbeck, died unexpectedly. The subsequent chairman, Prof. Dr. Klaus G. Lederer, tried one new managing director after another. The first, Dirk Rathjens, was fired after a short and turbulent phase during which relations between Attica and the yard became significantly strained. (After leaving HDW, Rathjens joined another North German shipbuilder, Flender Werft in Lübeck, where Attica subsequently ordered additional Superfast vessels, described below). At HDW, he was replaced by Jürgen Kennemann, but in short order he was superseded by Dieter Goerlitz, who was seconded from HDW's Naval Division. Fortunately for all concerned, Goerlitz showed his determination not only to build and deliver very good ships but also to try very hard to meet the agreed delivery times. Meanwhile, HDW's parent company, Babcock AG, was itself struggling financially. As Costis Stamboulelis remembers, during this period of managerial changes, such progress as was made on the vessels' construction was 'thanks to the devotion and persistence of a number of good and knowledgeable engineers in both the design and production departments.'

While the *Superfast V* and *Superfast VII* were being built in Germany, back on the Adriatic a very unfortunate incident took place on the *Superfast III* in November 1999 when a fire began in a truck trailer, parked on the lower vehicle deck. This spread to neighbouring vehicles, necessitating the evacuation by lifeboat of all 307 passengers and some of the 106 crew, while the others remained onboard to tackle the blaze. According to Costis Stamboulelis,

'The evacuation of the passengers was carried out in a very orderly fashion. Not only people, but also pets were taken care of – dogs being carried personally by the chief steward to their owners in the lifeboats. The fire was controlled and eventually put out by the crew who fought it with great courage and determination. The ship then proceeded under its own power to Hellenic Shipyards in Skaramanga. With many of the key Attica people in Kiel supervising the construction of the next Superfast vessels, contingency measures required to be made immediately. Myron Vergis, our Chief Electrical Engineer, left on a charter flight from Hamburg and boarded the vessel when close to Piraeus and I arrived in Skaramanga during the berthing manoeuver. When the vessel was safely berthed and the stern ramps were lowered, the first task was to empty the garages of all the trailers and trucks, most of which had been destroyed.'

During this grim and distressing process, the bodies of fourteen refugees from Kurdistan who were illegal stowaways in a truck trailer were found and it appeared that they had started the fire to try to cook food for themselves. The incident provoked a debate in Greece about port security. Once their bodies were recovered, the task of assessing the damage began. Meanwhile, Alexander Panagopoulos contacted and negotiated with the insurers and with various shipyards and contractors who might be able to repair the ship but as the damage was very substantial it was finally decided to send it to Blohm & Voss in Hamburg, a yard with great expertise in repairing badly damaged vessels. Attica's Superintendent Naval Architect, John Revelas, who was at that time in Kiel supervising at HDW, was appointed to manage the rebuilding project and joined the vessel in Greece where some temporary repairs were carried out to make it fit

to be sailed to Germany. As Costis Stamboulelis recalls:

'It so happened that the ship arrived in the Elbe estuary just as a storm was approaching. The river and the port of Hamburg were closed and it was necessary to ride out the big waves. On board the vessel, John Revelas was extremely anxious as he knew that parts of the steel structure had been badly weakened by the fire and that it would not withstand such continuous punishment. Alas, his anxiety caused him to suffer a heart attack the day after the ship had safely arrived at the yard. Fortunately, he was well looked after by the Hamburg doctors and medical staff and he fully recovered after three months.'

The repairs to the *Superfast III* also lasted for over three months and involved the replacement of 900 tons of steel and 70 kilometres of cabling, the installation of new electrical and hydraulic systems and the complete replacement of an internal lifting ramp between the lower and upper vehicle decks. Fortunately, the vessel was able to return to service, as good as new, in time for the 2000 summer season.

The fire on *Superfast III* led Attica's newbuilding team to decide to revise the specifications for the design of the vessels under construction in HDW. The most important change was to locate as much cabling as possible, including the major circuit cables, inside the casing rather than in the vehicle decks themselves. Another was to enable the operation of the drencher valves from the bridge. Myron Vergis recalls that there were 'long and heated discussions with HDW especially about passing the cables inside the casing, which they initially refused to do. They were finally convinced when they visited the damaged *Superfast III* at Blohm & Voss and saw for themselves the reason for our request.'

In Kiel, the sea trials of the *Superfast V* got off to a troublesome start as teething problems emerged – echoing the experience with the *Superfast III* in Finland. The most awkward of these was the failure of the Schelde reduction gears. This was surprising as they had performed very well on the *Superfast III* and *Superfast IV*. After a thorough investigation by the yard, it was decided to order new gears from a different supplier, Renk-Tacke, for both *Superfast V* and *Superfast VI*. The change of gears resulted in a considerable delay with the *Superfast V* in the end being the second vessel to be delivered in March 2001. The Schelde gears were kept on *Superfast VI* as they presented no problems during trials in February of the same year and so the second set of brand new Renk-Tacke gears was left at the yard when the vessel departed for Greece. The extra weight and delay to the *Superfast V* necessitated HDW in making a compensation payment

Top: The **Superfast VI** is seen arriving at Patras. *(Bruce Peter)*

Left: A stern-quarter view of the **Superfast VI** at Patras. *(Bruce Peter)*

to Attica Enterprises. According to Costis Stamboulelis, 'In the end, HDW did a wonderful job, albeit at considerable additional cost to themselves. The *Superfast V* and *Superfast VI* had superbly spacious and luxurious passenger accommodation which set even higher standards on the Adriatic than we were achieving already. At a time when I was briefly back in Athens, Pericles Panagopoulos said to me in a kind of confession "we certainly have not learned how to build less expensive ships"'.

The sudden decision to use the *Superfast VII* and *Superfast VIII* in the Baltic rather than the Mediterranean necessitated a quick change to the plans and specifications to give them ice class hull strength, the necessary amendment to the construction contracts being signed off at the end of March 1999. At the same time Attica ordered from HDW two further ice class vessels for Baltic service, the *Superfast IX* and *Superfast X*. The reason was that Alexander Panagopoulos had decided to open a second long Baltic route, this time between Germany and Sweden. With regard to the choice of Swedish port, there were several options, the only precondition agreed among Attica's team being that it should be somewhere in the vicinity of Stockholm so that the Superfast Ferries' speed advantage could be used to provide a schedule that was competitive in voyage duration and cost with driving to southern Sweden, then taking one of the short ferry crossings to Germany or Poland from Malmö, Ystad or Trelleborg. Attica representatives initially inspected Nynäshamn, which already had passenger terminal facilities for ferries to Poland and to the Swedish island of Gotland. Next, they made an unannounced visit to Södertälje, a nearby small freight ro-ro port close to substantial commercial vehicle factories from which new trucks and bus chassis were exported, as well as other manufactured items. There, they had an impromptu meeting with the Managing Director, Ingvar Wirén, from which they left with a positive impression of the its potential.

The four Baltic Superfast vessels were to measure 30,285 gt and accommodate just 626 passengers, all berthed in cabins, rather than the mix of berths and reclining seats of the Adriatic ships. To make the most efficient use of space in their consequently smaller superstructures, they would have an entirely different internal layout of the passenger decks. A horizontal subdivision of cabins and public rooms was selected, rather than vertical as on the earlier vessels. The main lounge faced forward, rather than aft, and the decks narrowed towards the stern. Although the range of indoor passenger facilities offered was broadly similar across the entire Superfast fleet, a major difference was that, in the Adriatic for much of the year, a lot of passenger activity took place outdoors, next to the swimming pool. This gave these vessels a particular cruise-style ambience and helped to disguise the fact that a large part of their internal volume was actually dedicated to the carriage of freight. Without poolside life, the Baltic Superfasts were much more similar to conventional ro-pax tonnage in northern Europe. Inboard, however, they were fitted with two saunas, plus massage rooms and a Jacuzzi; these facilities were vital for German and Finnish Baltic ferries and were appreciated by passengers and truck drivers alike.

With regard to Attica's interactions with the Baltic ports' managements, Costis Stamboulelis recalls that:

'In Rostock, Hanko and Södertälje we were fortunate in dealing with reasonable, open-minded and forward-looking port managers who were fully aware of the importance of efficient port operations and fully cooperative in designing with us and having constructed the necessary link spans for two-deck simultaneous loading and fully-covered passenger embarkation bridges, the example of which in Hanko was very long. Our naval architecture consultant, Holger Terpet of Knud E. Hansen A/S, provided highly detailed drawings of our planned vessels berthed bow first or stern first, with and without trim and at different draughts, to ensure that in every possible scenario all of the link spans would work perfectly. The order for the link span in Rostock was placed with Neptun Werft which was across the bay from the Superfast berthing pier. It was a magnificent, massive, heavy duty construction which worked perfectly well for loading the vessels via the bow. Subsequently observing their efficient loading, I could not but feel what a shame it was that we could not achieve anything similar in the Greek and Italian ports.'

Alexander Panagopoulos next planned to add a third north European route across the North Sea between Zeebrugge in Belgium and Rosyth in Scotland. Just like the Adriatic and Baltic Superfast services it too was relatively lengthy and would likewise require the ferries' high-speed to be exploited to enable passage times of under 20 hours' duration. The Scottish Government greatly anticipated the opening of Scotland's first direct ferry service to the European continent and gave the project's realisation considerable support. (A parallel between the Panagopouloses's pan-European approach in the ferry sector could be made with that of another Greek shipping tycoon, Stelios Haji-Ioannou, who in 1995 founded the budget airline easyJet and very quickly developed a network of routes covering much of the continent.)

Superfast was actually one of several Greek ferry companies to invest heavily in new tonnage during the boom years of the latter 1990s, aided by Greek and German banks suddenly being very willing to extend loans to finance the purchase of new vessels and even entire existing ferry operations on an unprecedented scale. In addition to the six new Superfast ships under construction at HDW, in August 1999, Attica Enterprises bought a large new shareholding in Strintzis Lines, representing 38.8 per cent of its overall capital. Shortly after, it acquired more Strintzis shares, meaning that its holding grew to 48.8 per cent. Strintzis already had recently placed its own orders for five large new ferries, two to be built in the Netherlands for cross-Adriatic service where they would be operating in competition with Superfast, and three for Greek domestic routes in the Aegean. Of the latter, one would be built in South Korea and the others in Greece. Now, in addition to its own rapid expansion programme for Superfast, Attica Enterprises also gained a large stake in these projects, which are described in a subsequent chapter.

Next, early in 2001, Attica Enterprises placed orders for a further two ferries, the 30,902 gt *Superfast XI* and *Superfast XII*, for delivery in the spring of the following year. The initial intention was that they would be used between Rosyth and Zeebrugge but, later on, it was decided instead that they would be deployed on the Adriatic between

Top: The **Superfast VII** amid winter ice off the Finnish port of Hanko. *(Attica Group)*

Above: The **Superfast IX** passes beneath the Forth Railway Bridge inbound to Rosyth. *(Attica Group)*

Right: The **Superfast VIII** is seen approaching Rostock. *(Bruce Peter collection)*

The lounge and cocktail bar on the **Superfast IX**. *(Bruce Peter)*

The spa area on the **Superfast IX**. *(Bruce Peter)*

Another view of the **Superfast IX**'s lounge. *(Bruce Peter)*

The a la carte restaurant on the **Superfast IX**. (*Bruce Peter*)

A standard outside cabin on the **Superfast IX**. (*Bruce Peter*)

One of the **Superfast IX**'s luxury suites, overlooking the bow. (*Attica Group*)

Top: Viewed from the Forth Road Bridge, the *Superfast IX* passes beneath parallel the Forth Railway Bridge towards the end of an overnight crossing from Zeebrugge to Rosyth. *(Bruce Peter)*

Above: In evening light, the *Superfast X* leaves Rosyth for Zeebrugge. *(Bruce Peter)*

Right: The *Superfast X* heads for Belgium amid the attractive scenery of the Firth of Forth. *(Bruce Peter)*

Patras, Igoumenitsa and Ancona. This time, the winning bid came from a different German shipyard, Flender Werft of Lübeck, which twenty-five years previously had built the fast and innovative North Sea ferries *Tor Britannia* and *Tor Scandinavia* – vessels which had first demonstrated the idea of running a long-haul service at speeds of over 25 knots.

The Superfasts built by HDW in Kiel provided ideal points of reference which Attica's management used as the basis for their negotiations with Flender Werft. The horizontal layout of public rooms and cabins was retained although the superstructure was extended further aft with the lifeboats placed towards the stern. In fact an aft lounge was only added to the general arrangement plan shortly before the contract was signed. The inclusion of couchettes and reclining seats gave a total passenger capacity of 1,427 of whom 774 were berthed, and there was also an outdoor swimming pool, sheltered by glazed screens, on the topmost passenger deck.

Although much of the overall design formula of the HDW vessels remained, there were, however, some significant though less visible changes in the specification, not least because in Adriatic service they would not require ice classed hulls. Another change was a fractional reduction in hull length. The reason was that when the previous Adriatic Superfast vessels, the *Superfast V* and *Superfast VI*,

had entered service, it was discovered that it was necessary to pay increased port fees because their length exceeded the ports' 200-metre pricing threshold. Consequently, Pericles Panagopoulos insisted that the new pair must be slightly shorter and so they were 199.99 metres long.

Furthermore, to cut costs and also to reduce complexity for the shipyard, it was decided to omit a bow door and hoistable car decks as there was obviously no chance of linkspans for bow-loading appearing any time soon in the Adriatic ports (hoistable car decks were however retrofitted on *Superfast XI* a decade later). The shipyard wanted additionally to omit bilge keels and put pressure on Costis Stamboulelis and his colleagues to strike them from the specification. This was however a breach of Pericles Panagopoulos's standing order to Stamboulelis since the days of construction of the *Crown Odyssey* never to accept a new passenger ship without bilge keels. The reason was that the cruise ship *Golden Odyssey* had not had these and he had deeply regretted their absence as increased rolling motion necessitating the use of the vessel's stabilisers with a detrimental effect upon fuel economy. Because bilge keels also slightly increase water resistance, the yard was worried that their presence would make it harder to attain the necessary contract speed – but they had not caused problems in this regard on the previous Superfasts.

Attica negotiated the order with Flender Werft's Managing Director, Martin Krause, and his colleague, Jürgen Hansen. The contract price was 200 million Euros and the yard expected to make a 20 million Euro loss, which its management felt was sustainable as constructing the Superfast vessels would enable continuity of turnover and employment for staff. When construction of the vessels was at an early stage, however, the former-HDW Managing Director, Dirk Rathjens, was brought in to take-over the leadership of yard. According to Attica's German shipbroker, Rimbert Harpain:

'We were all shocked when Mr Rathjens, with whom we had problems at HDW, came to take charge at Flender and, incidentally, this was also allegedly the opinion of the yard's union representatives. I remember that one of his first acts was to cancel contracts with major subcontractors which led to heavy delays and penalty payments. In those days Mr. Rathjens was already talking about a possible insolvency of the yard which was finally declared in June 2002. Apparently because of decisions made by the yard's management the losses on the Superfast contracts grew to 100 million Euros and led to its bankruptcy before the delivery of the second vessel.'

According to Costis Stamboulelis,

'The Flender people had followed closely the progress of the HDW Superfasts and were fully aware of the problems encountered there and the mistakes made which they were

The cafeteria on the **Superfast XI**. *(Apostolos Molindris)*

A dramatic aerial view of the **Superfast XI** at sea, showing the extensive sheltered areas of outside deck. *(Attica Group)*

The a la carte restaurant on the **Superfast XI**. *(Apostolos Molindris)*

A bow-quarter view of the **Superfast XI**. *(Attica Group)*

careful not to repeat. One mistake however was in the selection of an untried subcontractor for part of the interior outfitting. When the yard presented to us their preferred subcontractor for all the stair towers of the vessel, we stated our interest in getting to know him as we had never worked with him before. Our interior architect, Apostolos Molindris, visited his premises in Italy and was not satisfied with what he saw. We immediately informed the yard about our concern regarding his capacity to deliver, but they ignored our worries. The result was that much later on, when the public rooms, cabins and corridors were already at a very advanced stage of completion, the work in the stair towers was lagging far behind schedule and the subcontractor then walked away, leaving the spaces half finished. A new subcontractor was then called in to dismantle all that had been done until then and to start again from scratch at considerable extra cost to the yard, which could ill-afford the extra outlay.'

In spite of Flender Werft's financial problems, the two vessels went through successful sea trials and were completed to very high standards of quality and craftsmanship. In the end, Flender filed for insolvency shortly before the delivery of *Superfast XII* which was the last ever ship completed there.

According to the maritime industry newspaper *Fairtrade*, until that point, Flender had 'appeared to possess one of the healthiest order books, including three sophisticated ferry new buildings and three units of the largest container vessel type on order in Germany at that time. But the contract to build the ferries *Superfast XI* and *Superfast XII* proved to be a white elephant.' Dirk Rathjens told Fairplay that a major problem for Flender was that the yard was not technically equipped to carry out the Superfast orders.

The *Superfast VII* was delivered in May 2001 and, before entering service between Rostock and Hanko, was sent for a presentation visit to Rosyth to show dignitaries there what a future Superfast service would be like. The *Superfast VIII* joined the Rostock-Hanko route in July 2001. In January 2002, the *Superfast IX* inaugurated the Rostock-Södertälje service but as soon as operations commenced, the established ferry operators linking southern Swedish ports with Germany slashed their fares with the result that Superfast's operation, with its expensive new ships and relatively high fuel costs, suffered from a chronic lack of custom, meaning that there was no other option but to abandon it in April 2002 after just four months. A more fundamental long-term problem was that in any case north-south traffic, especially freight originating in the Stockholm area, used Sweden's excellent trunk roads and so there was no need for

coastal ferry duplication. For road hauliers, the advantage of driving south was that drivers could make best use of the allowable driving hours (recorded by tachograph) with their mandatory rest break coinciding with the ferry crossing. On the southern coasts of the Adriatic, by contrast, the roads were far from good and this gave ferry operators sailing from ports in northern and central Italy a big advantage. The brand new passenger terminal building that had been erected in Södertälje thereafter lay empty. Following the route's closure, the second vessel intended to operate on it, the *Superfast X*, instead temporarily entered service in February 2002 between Rostock and Hanko. For Attica, the Swedish experience proved costly but fortunately its Rostock-Hanko service proved to be a greater success.

According to Hercules Simitsidellis, the sudden popularity of the World Wide Web at the same time as the Baltic and North Sea Superfast routes were launched proved highly advantageous:

'Superfast was an early user of a web-based sales platform and passenger and cargo sales agents, specialising in selling ferry crossings, were appointed around the world to market and sell Superfast Ferries through the company's online reservation system. The Superfast website allowed customers to navigate and sense the "Superfast" experience, then immediately to proceed to make their reservation.

To compliment, and support the Head Office's commercial efforts in the field of marketing, sales and servicing for the Adriatic, Baltic and North Sea operations, Attica Premium offices were set up in Athens and Thessaloniki (Greece), Lübeck (Germany), Helsinki (Finland), Stockholm (Sweden), Zeebrugge (Belgium) and Rosyth (Scotland). Local travel industry professionals were recruited to man these Attica Premium offices, who acted as "ambassadors", using their knowledge to expand each regional market. Accessible and immediate confirmation of the reservation, a smooth check-in and an orderly embarkation to the vessel was part of the whole operational cycle.'

In May 2002, the *Superfast IX* and *Superfast X* inaugurated the new Rosyth-Zeebrugge route which, while certainly more successful than the one between Rostock and Södertälje, nonetheless suffered from similar problems in that Scottish drivers could with relative ease instead head south to ports on the Humber estuary, or even to those on the English Channel, instead of taking a direct ferry from Scotland. Besides, going immediately from zero capacity to two large

The reception area on the **Superfast XI** which featured a curved sweep of large windows set into a recess in the side of the superstructure. *(Apostolos Molindris)*

The forward-facing lounge on the **Superfast IX**. *(Apostolos Molindris)*

The **Superfast IX**'s aft lounge, overlooking the stern. *(Apostolos Molindris)*

A stairway on the **Superfast XI**. *(Apostolos Molindris)*

vessels, each providing 1,920 lane metres of parking space and 626 berths every night, was a tall order. Other successful ferry routes from the UK, by contrast, had tended to start with smaller vessels and to build up over time (the DFDS Newcastle-Ijmuiden service was a prime example of this approach). During the peak holiday season, fortunately, there was such great demand for berths that, when the *Superfast IX* and *Superfast X* subsequently were sent for overhaul at Fosen in Norway, additional ones were installed, raising the number to 728 berths in each. The problem was that during the remainder of the year, loadings were much lower and, throughout the year, the vessels' freight capacity was far less well utilised than had been expected. Besides, flying Greek officers and crew to and from the ships was a costly additional overhead.

The *Superfast XI* and *Superfast XII*, meanwhile, were completed by Flender Werft in July and October 2002. On the Patras-Igoumenitsa-Ancona route, they superseded the four-year-old *Superfast III* and

The two outdoor swimming pools, respectively for children and adults, on the **Superfast XI**. *(Attica Group)*

The funnel and part of the superstructure of the **Superfast XII**, as viewed from the quay at Piraeus. *(Bruce Peter)*

The **Spirit of Tasmania II**, ex **Superfast III**, is seen departing from Devonport for Hobart in Tasmania. For Australian service, most aspects of the Superfast identity were retained, although the upturned winglets on the funnel casing were truncated. *(Mitchell Bruce)*

Superfast IV, which were sold for a profit to TT Line of Melbourne, Australia, for service from there to Hobart in Tasmania – a challenging stretch of sea prone to exceptionally high waves. The vessels were renamed the *Spirit of Tasmania I* and *Spirit of Tasmania II* but where otherwise little altered as TT Line introduced its version of the Superfast concept on the other side of the world with even the original livery largely intact. The only major change, in fact, was the cutting off of the upturned winglets on the fins protruding from the funnel casing – a necessary modification to protect Superfast's trademark design. These sales were the first of a succession by Superfast over the ensuing decade as it quickly was forced to alter its fleet disposition and route network in the face of steeply increasing fuel costs and the reconstruction of the Balkans Highway through Croatia, which brought about a levelling off of cross-Adriatic freight

and car traffic.

In June 2003, one of the original pair of Superfast vessels, the *Superfast II*, was also sold to TT Line of Tasmania to join the former *Superfast III* and *Superfast IV* in its fleet, enabling a new direct service from Sydney to Hobart to be tried; for this purpose, the vessel was renamed the *Spirit of Tasmania III*. Less than a year later, the *Superfast I* was sold too – but this time the buyer was Grimaldi Lines, owned by the Italian ship owner Guido Grimaldi and his son, Emanuel. The vessel was placed in service on a relatively lengthy western Mediterranean route between Civitavecchia, the port nearest to Rome, and Barcelona as the *Eurostar Roma*. Not only were the funnel winglets cut off, but the vessel was repainted in Grimaldi's dark blue hull and funnel livery, giving a distinctly different external impression from before.

Above: A stern-quarter view of the **Spirit of Tasmania II** showing the plated in rear section of the upper vehicle deck to protect from heavy seas washing over. *(Mitchell Bruce)*

Left: The **Spirit of Tasmania**, ex-**Superfast II**, is seen leaving Sydney with the famous Opera House in the background during the brief and ultimately unsuccessful attempt at reviving the service between there and Devonport in 2004-2006. *(Bruce Peter collection)*

CHAPTER SIX

BLUE STAR FERRIES

When in 1999, Attica Enterprises bought a 48.8 per cent shareholding in Strintzis Lines it was acquiring a ferry company with a history far longer than that of Superfast. Strintzis Lines was a family-run ferry business, the owners of which lived on the island of Kefalonia in the Ionian Sea off the Peloponnese coast. Indeed, the Strintzis family's shipping interests could be traced back to the mid- nineteenth century, when Captain Antonis Strintzis purchased a small cargo vessel, the *St Giovanni*, to trade among the Ionian Islands – which at that time were under British rule – and the mainland of Greece. At that time, raisins were a major export cargo from the islands. Subsequent generations of the family-owned vessels not only traded in the eastern Mediterranean but also in the Black Sea. In 1953, the need to rebuild Kefalonian villages after an earthquake led the Strinzis family to focus their shipping operations on bringing materials to the island to assist with this work and was also the beginning of their regular services there from Patras. In 1960 Dimitrios and Antonis Strintzis decided to enter the ferry business, purchasing a 23-year-old passenger and cargo steamer, which was rebuilt at Perama with a capacity for 40 cars and 350 passengers. This

entered service in 1961 as the *Agios Gerasimos* between Patras, Kefalonia and Ithaki and was was one of the few car-carrying ferries operating in Greek waters at that time. In 1963, the Strintzis brothers ordered a purpose-built ferry from the Zervas Shipyard at Perama for use on the Aegean from Piraeus. The 2,375 grt *Kefallinia*, which cost five million drachmas, was an ambitious project for the Strintzis brothers as well as for the builder and their financiers but, once in service in 1965, it proved sufficiently successful that another new ferry was added in 1972 – the 3,350 grt *Ionion*, built by Hellenic General Enterprises, also of Perama. The 21 million drachma cost of the project was financed by the National Investment Bank for Industrial Development and the construction was supervised by Antonis Strintzis's son, Panagis, who was a marine engineering graduate but hitherto had worked on ocean-going ships, rather than ferries. At a time when Greek domestic ferry operations were dominated by second hand tonnage, the two Strintzis vessels were unusual in being purpose-designed for routes to the central Aegean islands, where there was a rapidly-growing tourist trade.

In 1976, Strintzis Lines entered the international cross-Adriatic ferry trade between Greece and Italy, having purchased for this purpose the 1964-built, 3,625 grt *Leif Erikson* from the Canadian National ferry company, for which the vessel had most recently operated on Canada's Atlantic seaboard between Nova Scotia and Newfoundland. Originally, however, she had been built in West Germany by Werft Nobiskrug of Rendsburg as the *Prins Bertil* for the Swedish ferry operator Lion Ferry's route between Halmstad in Sweden and Århus in Denmark and her design was by Knud E. Hansen A/S – the same firm as later produced plans for the Panagopoulos-owned Royal Cruise Line fleet and for Superfast. Strintzis renamed her as the *Ionian Star* and placed her in service between Patras and Igoumenitsa in Greece and Ancona in Italy. The fact that her service speed was just over 20 knots and that she had a substantial, unobstructed, double-height vehicle deck for freight gave Strintzis a clear advantage in this market over the incumbent operators, Hellenic Mediterranean Lines, Adriatica Line and Karageorgis Line, whose ferries were both slower and had far less car

The **Ionian Sta**r was Strintzis Lines' first ferry in Adriatic service from 1976 onwards. *(Bruce Peter collection)*

The ***Ionian Galaxy***, which was acquired from Japan then extensively-rebuilt, brought a superior standard to Strintzis Lines' cross-Adriatic service. *(Bruce Peter collection)*

In the 1980s and 90s, Strintzis Lines' fleet consisted of a very wide diversity of converted second-hand ferries, the ***Delos*** being the former SNCF Dover Strait vessel ***Valençay***. *(Ferry Publications Library)*

deck capacity.

One year after the *Ionian Star* entered service, Panagis Strintzis's cousin, Gerasimos, who had worked at Strintzis Lines since 1972, became its managing director while Panagis continued to deal with technical and operational matters. Thereafter, it was Gerasimos who guided the company through two decades of rapid expansion, during which it grew into one of Greece's leading and most respected ferry operators.

With the *Ionian Star*, Strintzis found a successful operational formula, but the fact that each crossing took a day and a half meant that departures from each end port could only be offered every four days. In 1981, a second vessel was acquired in the form of the 1958-built 3,670 grt French SNCF Dover Strait car ferry *Compiegne* which became the *Ionian Glory*. During the first half of the 1980s, Strintzis added several more second hand ferries to both their Adriatic and Aegean ferry fleets; in 1985-86 the former saw the introduction of two additional ex-SNCF cross-Channel vessels, the 2,286 grt *Villandry* and *Valencay* of 1965, which respectively became the *Delos* and *Eptanisos*. (The former was bought via another Greek ferry operator, Agapitos Bros, while the latter was acquired directly from SNCF.) In the same year, Strintzis also purchased the 4,849 grt B&I Line Irish Sea ferry *Leinster* of 1969, renaming her the *Ionian Sun*; she was a near-sister of the *Ionian Star*, ex *Prins Bertil*. In the following year, a much more ambitious purchase was made in the form of a large Japanese ferry, the 17,691 grt *Arkas*, which had been built in 1972 by Setoda Zoshensho Co. Ltd of Setoda for the Japanese coastal ferry operator,

Taiheiyo Enkai Kisen of Nagoya. In terms of passenger accommodation, Japanese ferries have very different types of facilities from European ones – open dormitories for sleeping and communal bathhouses, for example – so it was Strintzis's plan to carry out a major reconstruction in Greece into what would become arguably the first ever luxury cruise-ferry to trade between Greece and Italy with space for 1,612 passengers and no fewer than 600 cars – many more than on any of the existing ferries in the region. The conversion was completed in 1988 and the vessel entered service as the *Ionian Galaxy* to considerable acclaim. In 1989, Strintzis purchased its sister, the *Albireo*, which was given an even more thorough-going transformation, joining the fleet in 1990 as the *Ionian Island*. Although the pair were economical to operate and had superior passenger facilities – including an outdoor swimming pool, discotheque, cinema and casino – their service speed was a mere 19 knots, meaning that they offered the same slow two-night passage times as before. For five years – until the advent of Superfast – they were widely regarded as the best ships in the Greece-Italy trade, however.

Next, Strintzis Lines added to the fleet two late-1960s-vintage 5,223 grt former-Italian ferries that latterly had been operating on the Red Sea between Egypt, Jordan and Saudi Arabia. Renamed as the *Ionian Harmony* and *Ionian Sea*, they had originally been built in 1967 and 1968 by Italcantieri of Castellammare di Stabia for service between the Italian mainland and Sardinia as the *Canguro Verde* and *Canguro Bruno*. Unfortunately, they were even slower than the *Ionian Galaxy* and *Ionian Island*, being capable of just 16 knots on average. To bolster Strintzis Lines' Aegean operations, meanwhile, the 7,454 grt, 21-knot Japanese ferry *Dai-san Izu* – which had been built in 1972 by Hashihama Dockyard Co, Ltd of Imabari as the *Cassiopeia* – was acquired in 1991 from its initial Greek owner, Minoan Lines, and substantially rebuilt at Perama as the *Superferry* for use on the Rafina-Andros-Tinos-Mykonos-Syros route. Shortly after, the 1974-built, 5,052 grt, 22-knot Belgian cross-Channel ferry *Prins Laurent* was purchased in 1992 and, following a major renovation, was placed on the same service as the *Superferry 2*. In 1991, the *Superferry* was chartered to Swansea-Cork Ferries for summer service across the Irish Sea – a rare instance at that time of a Greek-owned ferry operating in northern Europe, but also a harbinger of events to come. Indeed, two years thereafter, Strintzis Lines took over the route and continued to operate it seasonally with the *Superferry* until 1998.

Back on the Adriatic, meanwhile, the outbreak of civil war in Yugoslavia in 1991 had led Strintzis Lines to focus increasingly on freight traffic as there was now a considerable increase in the number of trucks requiring transporting, especially between Italian ports and Igoumenitsa. To help accommodate this growing trade, in 1994 Strintzis bought a recently-completed Italian freight ferry, the 14,398 gt *Via Ligure*, which had been constructed by the modern Dutch shipyard of Van der Giessen de Noord Krimpen aan der Ijssel but had not been a commercial success in its initial deployment in Italian coastal service. Strintzis had the vessel rebuilt with additional passenger accommodation and placed her in Adriatic service as the *Ionian Star*. Attica Enterprises' 17 per cent shareholding in Strintzis

Lines – worth 3,000 million drachma – enabled the company to make this comparatively costly acquisition and also to finance the subsequent rebuilding. Later in 1994, Strintzis gained a public listing on the Athens Stock Exchange, which suddenly gave it access to substantial new sources of capital to invest in many more ferries. Indeed, it was the first Greek ferry company with an operational fleet to gain such a listing (Attica Enterprises' Superfast service was yet to commence).

For the comparatively short route between Patras and Kefalonia, in 1995 Strintzis made yet another purchase from Japan in the form of the twenty-year-old 3,924 grt *Venus*, which had been built by Naikai Shipbuilding & Engineering of Innoshima, and upon arrival in Greece, as was usual practice, was rebuilt at Perama before being redeployed by Strintzis Lines as the *Kefalonia*. Thus, by the latter 1990s, Strintzis had amassed a very big fleet of converted second hand ferries of various shapes, sizes, origins and vintages. Their next acquisition followed in 1996 in the form of the sturdy and capacious Australian-built 6,374 grt freight ferry *Bass Trader*, which dated from 1975 and was likewise rebuilt in Greece with additional superstructure, becoming the *Ionian Bridge*. By then, Superfast was up and running and, rather than attempting to compete in terms of speed and luxury, Strintzis decided to switch strategy to offer instead a budget passenger service and to continue to expand freight operations. Gerasimos Strintzis also decided that the best long-term solution for Strintzis would be to follow Attica Enterprises' example and to commence its own new building programme. While this

The **Superferry**, another rebuilt Japanese ferry, was used both in the Aegean and on the Irish Sea between Swansea and Cork. *(Bruce Peter collection)*

The Italian-built **Ionian Sea** was bought third-hand from an Egyptian owner for Aegean services. *(Bruce Peter collection)*

The **Superferry 2**, formerly the Belgian **Prince Lauren**t, proved to be an excellent purchase and was given a thorough rebuild before entering Aegean service from Rafina. Here, it is seen at Paros. *(Bruce Peter)*

The Japanese-built ro-pax ferry **Ionian Sky** departs Venice for Greece; the Blue Ferries livery was briefly applied to all of Strintzis Lines' older ships before Blue Star Ferries became the standard identity for the entire fleet. *(Bruce Peter collection)*

scheme was developed, further second hand freight-orientated ferries were purchased.

Strintzis Lines' third freighter, the Japanese-built 11,097 grt *Sunflower Sapporo* of 1974, was added in 1998 as the *Ionian Victory*. A fourth acquisition also from Japan was the 16,725gt, 23-knot *Varuna*, a well-equipped ten-year old ro-pax ferry with both a substantial vehicle deck capacity and extensive passenger accommodation. The vessel had been constructed by Japan's leading ferry builder, Mitsubishi Heavy Industries of Shimonoseki for Higashi Nihon Ferry; Strintzis Lines planned to name the ship *Superferry Hellas* and to add her to its burgeoning cross-Adriatic operation. Although the Yugoslav War had ended, the Balkans Highway was as yet not fully reinstated, meaning that high freight volumes would continue into the new millennium.

Meanwhile, projects were commenced to commission fast, purpose-built ferry tonnage, not only for cross-Adriatic routes, but also for Strintzis Lines' services from Patras to Kefalonia and from Piraeus and Rafina to the Aegean islands. 5,000 million drachma was raised on the Athens Stock Exchange to enable these projects to be brought to fruition. A first move was to order a pair of passenger-only catamarans of the Norwegian Westmarin-type, the first of which, named the *Sea Jet 1*, was built in Sweden by Oskarshamn Varv and delivered in 1995 to link Rafina with the popular tourist islands of Andros, Tinos and Mykonos in the central Aegean. The second, known as the *Sea Jet 2* and built by Båtservice Industrier of Mandal in Norway, followed in 1998 and was placed in service between Piraeus, Poros, Hydra and Spetises.

For its Adriatic routes, Strintzis decided that the best solution would be to provide an alternative to Superfast's service from Patras to Ancona by instead introducing a high-speed and high-quality ferry route from Patras to Brindisi in the south of Italy. This would enable Strintzis to offer the shortest crossing between the two countries – a mere overnight hop. Having been impressed by the quality of the *Ionian Star*, ex-*Via Ligure*, in 1995 Strintzis began discussions with Van der Giessen de Noord in the Netherlands as the yard already had been touting a concept design for a 27-knot ro-pax ferry type. In recent years, it had also produced numerous significant passenger and freight ferries, most recently for Irish Ferries and so it had gained a great deal of practical experience with vessels of this type. Although the yard quickly produced a satisfactory design solution for Strintzis, nearly three years elapsed before the necessary financial and other arrangements were in place to enable the project to proceed. Finally, in 1998, orders were placed for two 29,415 gt ferries – to be named the *Superferry Atlantic* and the *Superferry Pacific*. Powered by four MAN 8-cylinder diesels, their high-speed would mean less need for cabin berths, only 430 being provided out of a total passenger capacity of 1,600 – although their vehicle decks were similarly arranged to those of the Superfast fleet with 1,745 lane metres. The upper level had large circular cut-outs in the shell plating for natural ventilation and also to save weight. The Van der Giessen yard used a very efficient modular construction system, enabling the blocks for the second vessel to be prepared while the first was taking shape on the launch way. The vessels were due for delivery in June and July 2000.

Blue Star Jets' *Sea Jet 2* manoeuvres off the quay at Mykonos.
(Bruce Peter)

A stern-quarter view of the **Blue Horizon**, which was purchased by Strintzis Lines from Japan and remains in the present Blue Star Ferries fleet. *(Bruce Peter)*

Almost simultaneously, Strintzis additionally ordered three smaller ferries for Greek domestic routes. The smallest of these was a 10,193 gt, 1,238-passenger, 365-lane metre vessel for operation between Patras and Kefalonia to be named *Superferry Ithaki*. It was designed by the Finnish consultant naval architects, Deltamarin, and ordered from the Daewoo Shipbuilding & Heavy Machinery Ltd of Okpo in South Korea. With a 24-knot speed, it would offer not only greater comfort but also shorter passage times between the Strintzis family's home island and the mainland. Deltamarin also designed for Strintzis two somewhat larger and faster domestic ferries measuring 14,717 gt, accommodating 1,800 passengers and capable of 27 knots and these were ordered from the Hellenic Shipyards of Skaramanga in Greece for routes from Piraeus to the central and eastern Aegean islands (Strintzis had an option to have built a third example there, but this was never exercised). To be named the *Superferry Mykonos* and *Superferry Chios*, the pair were intended effectively to 'shrink' the Aegean, making return sailings in each 24-hour period where the existing ferries on the routes could only manage single ones. Ordering Aegean ferries in Greece was a return to Strintzis's original approach for its first ferries of the 1960s and early-1970s. All three vessels were – like the ones from Van der Giessen – expected to enter service in the millennium year, but while Daewoo made rapid progress with their example, the Hellenic Shipyards rapidly fell behind schedule.

While construction of all five new ferry projects was advancing at variable rates in the Netherlands, South Korea and Greece, in the autumn of 1999, Attica Enterprises gained a controlling stake in

Strintzis Lines. Although Gerasimos Strintzis remained as its head, the involvement of Attica led to a major re-think with regard to the vessels' deployment and brand identity. Furthermore, Alexander Panagopoulos decided that, rather than Strintzis Lines continuing to trade under its existing name and colours, it should be given a new image with wider appeal, commensurate in terms of style with that of Superfast. As feelings of being European were running high in Greece at that time, he decided to combine the European Union's yellow and blue colours with a new brand name 'Blue Star Ferries.' Blue, of course, also referenced Greek seafaring traditions and in addition these colours were the complementary primary shades to Superfast's bright red livery. As Costis Stamboulelis recalls,

'Alexander Panagopoulos and I were sitting in Apostolos Molindris's office, trying out various star shapes. Alex did not want just an ordinary idle star as used by many other shipping companies. He wanted a dynamic shape of a moving star and, after many trials, we arrived at the Blue Star we see today on all the company's vessels.

The Blue Star brand required a more sophisticated implementation strategy in comparison with that of Superfast because there were a variety of different spheres of operation and many more destinations, meaning that a vast amount of marketing material and new signage and displays for travel agents' shops needed to be made and distributed. The Superfast brand had been relatively easy to implement for reservations

The **Blue Star Ithaki** is seen while under construction at the Daewoo shipyard at Okpo in South Korea from which the large tankers berthed to the rear were more typical outputs. *(Bruce Peter collection)*

and sales because all the ships went from the Greek mainland to the Italian mainland and vice versa. Consequently, potential passengers booking anywhere in Europe simply had to say they wanted to travel to Greece with Superfast and that was all.'

The new identity initially had two versions; the older, second hand Strintzis ferries which were shortly to be phased out would henceforth trade as 'Blue Ferries' with 'Blue Star Ferries' applied only to the new ones. All of the ships were to be renamed with the prefix 'Ionian' replaced by 'Blue'.

The forthcoming Van der Giessen-built cross-Adriatic vessels would not only have different names – *Blue Star 1* and *Blue Star 2* – but also entirely different interiors, designed by the interior architect of the latest Superfast ships, Apostolos Molindris. Already, the Dutch builder had commissioned a Danish architect, Claus Horn, who had previously designed interiors for Irish Ferries' vessels built there, to carry out the work and had begun to order inventory based on his designs. The Panagopouloses judged what had been agreed upon by Strintzis to be insufficiently luxurious, however, and they insisted upon

upgrading to the same standards as on the Superfast fleet. This also reflected their decision that, instead of only shuttling back and forth between Brindisi and Patras, the two vessels would instead be used on a longer triangular service from Ancona via Brindisi to Patras, enabling freight to board at two Italian ports with a coastal voyage between to remove traffic from the motorway. Thus, so far as voyage duration was concerned, they would be offering a cruise-ferry service which would need to be commensurate with the Superfast routes. According to Costis Stamboulelis,

'Van der Giessen de Noord was a good shipyard, staffed with very experienced designers, naval architects and engineers, who – in the absence of particular requirements of the owners – were able to produce a good quality ship at the least possible cost. It therefore came as no surprise to us that they got very worried when Attica became the major shareholder of Strintzis Lines.

When Pericles Panagopoulos and I went to Van der Giessen for the first time, the future *Blue Star 1* was in an advanced stage of construction on the covered slipway. The head of Strintzis

Lines' supervision team, Captain Alexandros Papadeas, gave us a tour of the ship. Apart from the machinery spaces, the garages and passenger decks were only steel, piping and some ducting and cabling and it all looked very well done – sometimes too well. I was amazed by the evenness of the plating of Deck 7 where the public rooms were to be located. Not the slightest buckling was to be seen anywhere, but this was because the entire deck – being the first accommodation deck above the garage – was covered with a special very thick type of floating floor which fulfilled the fire insulation requirements. We at Attica had always specified that fire insulation was to be placed on the underside of the deck which is much more difficult for the yard to install. As we found out, no such provision had been made in the Dutch specification, so naturally the yard chose the easier way.

When we told them that we wanted a different interior design from the one produced by Claus Horn, there was panic. All the wall panels and doors had already been ordered on the basis of the 50 mm thick floating floor, so any change would result in considerable additional cost and delay. They obviously had a point we could not ignore so it was agreed that materials that were already delivered to the yard would be kept. We also had to maintain the location of certain rooms such as the galley and the provision rooms where hardware installation had already begun. Taking into account these constraints, Apostolos Molindris produced new layouts and colour schemes, different linings, floor coverings, furnishings and fabrics with the intention of making the vessels appear more cruise-like.

Attica's Captain George Kazepidis was appointed as the head of our site office which was otherwise manned by captains, superintendent engineers and electricians from Strintzis Lines. Although I was in Kiel supervising our projects there for Superfast, I had the daily contact with both Van der Giessen's Project Manager and our own people there, as well as with Apostolos Molindris in Athens and many queries were addressed in an orderly and efficient manner. In addition, Gerasimos Strintzis, Apostolos Molindris and I made regular visits during the construction of the two vessels to inspect the progress being made and resolve with the yard whatever issues had arisen. The construction was carried out with remarkable speed and efficiency and, in the end, despite the changes, there was little delay to the completion schedule.

We all attended the sea trials which took a little longer than intended and had to be repeated mostly to check that some vibration problems had been remedied by the fitment of additional stiffening. One evening towards the end of these on the *Blue Star 2*, Gerasimos Strintzis cooked spaghetti with tomato sauce for us and we thus inaugurated the a la carte restaurant with a private celebratory meal – though oddly the spaghetti was Japanese, coming in wooden boxes which our Dutch hosts had found among the provisions.'

The design of *Blue Star 1* and *Blue Star 2* earned very high praise from ferry industry commentators on account of their operational performance and high-capacity relative to their size (their length was the maximum that could be accommodated in many European ferry ports, not only those in Greece). One particularly admired feature of the passenger accommodation was the big square side windows of the public rooms which went practically from floor to ceiling and resulted in a very airy and fresh interior ambience. (Some years later, Stamboulelis and his colleagues specified the same design on the subsequent new Blue Star vessels, the *Blue Star Delos* and *Blue Star Patmos*, described below.)

As for Blue Star Ferries' South Korean new building, apart from gaining the modified name of *Blue Star Ithaki*, construction had already reached such an advanced stage it was impossible to make any modifications and so work progressed without change and the original intended interiors by the Athens-based architect, Panos Georganas, were installed. Rather than connecting Patras and Kefalonia, as had been planned, however, it was decided the vessel should be placed instead on a more lucrative route to the central Aegean islands from Rafina with daily calls as Syros, Paros, Naxos, Ios, Santorini and return.

With regard to the two ferries ordered by Strintzis from the Hellenic Shipyards in Skaramanga and originally intended to be named *Superferry Mykonos* and *Superferry Chios*, following Attica's acquisition of Strintzis and Costis Stamboulelis's initial visit to Van der Giessen to assess progress there on the eventual *Blue Star 1* and *Blue Star 2*, he made a brief fact-finding trip to the yard in Greece.

He found that the hull for the first of the vessels being built there was afloat and the steelwork for the superstructure had been constructed up to Deck 5, but very little progress had been made on the second one relative to what was stipulated in the construction schedule. This stagnation was mostly a consequence of ongoing industrial action by various shipyard workers' trade unions which did not appear likely to be resolved any time soon. Moreover, the procurement process arranged by the shipyard was unusually complicated. Although Deltamarin had produced the initial design,

The newly-introduced **Blue Star Ithaki** is seen arriving at Paros, one of the islands of the central Cyclades that the vessel brought within easier reach of Piraeus. *(Bruce Peter)*

Onboard, the **Blue Star Ithaki** had comfortable but relatively high-density accommodation, typified by this lounge area. *(Bruce Peter collection)*

The **Blue Star Ithaki**'s forward-facing observation lounge had an extra half-deck of height and large windows overlooking the bow. *(Bruce Peter collection)*

The newly-launched **Blue Star 2** with the **Blue Star 1** astern at the outfitting berth at the Van der Giessen shipyard in March 2000. *(Rob de Visser)*

A large reclining seat lounge on the **Blue Star 1**; for budget overnight travel, facilities such as this represented a great advance over the 'deck class' of previous generations of Adriatic ferry. *(Apostolos Molindris)*

Part of the Red Wine a la carte restaurant on the **Blue Star 2**. *(Bruce Peter)*

the yard had entrusted its development and the preparation of all construction drawings to naval architecture consultants in Romania. The detailed drawings for the outfitting work were prepared by a third external agent and, in the yard itself there was only one person, with whom Stamboulelis and Molindris had meetings, who had to coordinate all of the work.

As a result of there being arguably too many suppliers of drawings and insufficient coordination, Stamboulelis and his colleagues began to notice various design and construction mistakes. The purchasing department had placed orders for equipment based on insufficient and often incorrect information – for example, the stern ramp was ordered before the optimal length of the vessels' ducktail sponsons were finally determined by model tests. The result was that the ramp was too short, meaning that it would not be able to reach the quay and would need to be replaced. Attica established a site supervision office, headed by John Revelas, who had fully recovered from his heart problems and was happy to be working close to his home and his family. Apostolos Molindris was appointed to tackle the design of the interiors. As Costis Stamboulelis recalls,

'We wanted to make changes, to make the two ships suitable for different routes and trades, but were restricted by the purchasing rush that had preceded our involvement and by the design work already carried out. There were however certain matters upon which we insisted and one of them was the provision of lifeboats. As originally conceived by Strintzis, the vessels were for use only on particular domestic routes and so only needed to have marine evacuation systems. Pericles Panagopoulos was not of the same opinion; he wanted to have ferries capable of being certified for employment on many different routes, including short international ones. "A passenger ship without lifeboats is not a proper passenger ship" he said and there would be no argument about it. It was too late to do anything on the first vessel without dismantling much of the construction already completed, but it was indeed possible to amend the second. New drawings were prepared, new calculations were made and four lifeboats were provided.'

Revised completion dates in 2001 were agreed but when the vessels still were not ready even a year thereafter a disappointing alternative solution was reached to annul the contracts and Attica was paid compensation.

A couple of years later, a fresh attempt was made to interest Attica in completing the vessels. Since the cancellation of the earlier

The forward-facing Observation Lounge on the **Blue Star 1**, the exceptionally large windows of which drew favourable comments from ferry design professionals and passengers alike. *(Apostolos Molindris)*

contracts, the Greek government had entered into an agreement with Howaldtswerke Deutsche Werft to build four new submarines for the Hellenic Navy. The first of these was to be constructed at HDW's shipyard in Kiel and the remaining three were to be built at the Hellenic Shipyards facility at Skaramanga. Howaldtswerke Deutsche Werft gained control of the Greek yard and Attica's old acquaintance from the HDW Superfast projects, Dieter Goerlitz, was appointed as its new CEO. Although Goerlitz was primarily responsible for the submarine programme, when he saw the partially-completed ferry hulls lying there and also the warehouses filled with all kinds of equipment and materials which had been purchased for them, he thought he should do something about these valuable abandoned items and so he got in touch with Attica's management to persuade them to re-engage with the projects. According to Costis Stamboulelis,

'Mr Goerlitz promised that he would be very accommodating to our requirements and we would be able to complete both vessels at a very attractive price, although if my recollection is correct, his preference was to sell everything to us and let us take it all away and complete the construction anywhere we liked. Negotiations carried on for some time, but our

A wide seating arcade on the **Blue Star 2**; the wall decorations by Apostolos Molindris are reminiscent of the approach used by Michaelis Katzourakis on Royal Cruise Line's ships of the 1970s. *(Bruce Peter)*

The cafeteria servery on the **Blue Star 1**. *(Apostolos Molindris)*

management was split in two between those in favour and those against this course of action. For the record I was in favour but in the end those against were in the majority and so Mr Goerlitz's offer was rejected.'

Eventually, the vessels were sold to another major Greek ferry operator, Minoan Flying Dolphins, which used subcontractors to complete them and they entered service in 2005 and 2007 respectively under the Hellenic Seaways brand as the *Nissos Mykonos* and *Nissos Chios* (see below).

In the interim, the *Blue Star Ithaki*, *Blue Star 1* and *Blue Star 2* entered service between June and July 2000. Although all three were well received, it was the *Blue Star Ithaki* which made the biggest impact, being the first fast conventional ferry connecting the Aegean islands. Its nimble manoeuvring ability enabled very fast turnarounds at each port of call, between which it sprinted smoothly and efficiently. Inboard, there were modern and comfortable saloons – a notable feature being the forward-facing observation lounge, in which there was a void space behind the front of the superstructure with large panoramic windows filling most of the height of two decks; this feature was surely inspired by recent Baltic Sea cruise ferries, in the design of which Deltamarin's naval architects had also been involved. Rather than a cafeteria, there was a fast food bar because typical voyages were now so short that it was expected that most passengers would only want snack food. The outside decks, meanwhile, were

sheltered with a tensile awning. If there was a criticism of the vessel, it was that she was too small to cope with the demand she generated and was often crowded and with a frenetic atmosphere on board – a victim of her own popularity. Nonetheless, for those willing to pay, it was possible to book one of a small number of *en suite* cabins to escape the busy public rooms and circulation areas. The owners were obviously satisfied, though, because very quickly two more examples of the type were ordered for delivery in the early-summer of 2002; these were the 10,438 gt, 1,500-passenger *Blue Star Paros* and *Blue Star Naxos*, which were for use on popular Aegean routes from Piraeus. According to Costis Stamboulelis:

'One October 2000 evening in Kiel, Pericles Panagopoulos telephoned me to request that I come back to Athens to discuss and agree with the Daewoo people the specification of two sister vessels to the *Blue Star Ithaki*. I told him I would be there the next day, but I also asked him if he really intended to repeat the layout of the *Ithaki* which I thought it could be improved and made more appealing by allowing in it as much natural light as possible. When he replied in the affirmative, I caught myself telling him in a rather loud voice that he could not be serious. I said to him "Mr. Panagopoulos, this is a bad layout and we can do much better", but he was adamant in his decision.

By sheer coincidence Apostolos Molindris was in Kiel for one of his regular inspections of the Superfasts and he was going to travel with me back to Greece. I told him we had to submit a new proposal for the *Ithaki* sisters and we would have to do it very quickly. I had the general arrangement plan of the *Ithaki* with me, so the next day on the plane we opened it on the fold-down tables. Apostolos got out his A3 tracing paper and we started changing the layout of the public rooms and of all the accommodation decks. When back in our office, we presented to Mr. Panagopoulos a very rough freehand drawing spread over 3 or 4 transparent sheets attached to each other with Sellotape. I must say I was surprised when he told us that he liked the new arrangement. He simply said "Put it all on one piece of paper even in this rough form and present it to the Koreans". This was going to be one day later and so Apostolos had to rush to prepare as good a drawing as he could. Another fully accurate one would need to be prepared after Daewoo agreed to the proposed changes, however.'

Whereas the *Blue Star Ithaki* had been designed for the short route to Kefalonia, for the route to the Cyclades, the two new vessels were would need to have an adequate number of passenger cabins. To enable this, practically the entire crew accommodation including the crew mess rooms was shifted to the rear part of the upper vehicle deck. The reduced car capacity on this deck was compensated by the installation of hoistable platform car decks on the main deck. A total thirty-five passenger cabins were provided on the deck above the public rooms, offering 120 berths, but this was later reduced when eight cabins in the aft part were converted into reclining seat lounges. As the shipyard's designers became concerned about the impact of these changes upon the vessel's the lightship weight, it was decided to omit the bow door and ramp, which the Blue Star Ithaki was equipped with, thus sparing a considerable weight.

Rather than repeat the strictly rectilinear arrangement of the public rooms on the *Blue Star Ithaki*, to give a greater variety of ambience, Molindris's reorganisation followed a similar approach to that used on the Superfast vessels. The large forward-facing lounge was given a circular layout and the aft lounges and catering facilities were reorganised into a series of smaller and more intimate spaces. The colours and materials were also very similar to those of the Superfast fleet, with the result that passengers first crossing the Adriatic and then continuing to the Cyclades with ferry trips under each Attica brand would enjoy a similar level of experience on both sea legs. Costis Stamboulelis recalls what happened with regard to the contract negotiations:

'The South Korean delegation arrived the next day, pretty sure that we were going to sign a contract for two more 'Ithakis' and so they were startled when they saw the revised interior arrangement, but nonetheless displayed an admirable adaptability to the new situation. In fact, the entire specification was revised. Needless to say, the many changes caused considerable anxiety to the head of the delegation who was smoking one cigarette after the other. There were no rules about not smoking in offices in those days, but at a certain point Alexander Panagopoulos was visibly suffering and could not take it any longer so he requested everyone please to stop smoking in the meeting room.'

In the end, the specification was agreed, proper drawings were prepared and the contract was signed at an increased price. Having two more new buildings in Korea simultaneously with all the other new buildings in Germany and Greece stretched the capacity of Attica's supervisory teams to the very limit, nonetheless they managed to attend as well as possible to all of them. According to Stamboulelis, it helped greatly that Daewoo's people were very efficient and cooperative and they delivered highly satisfactory vessels in just 18 months.

Attica's site office in Okpo was headed by John Revelas, assisted by Superintendent Engineer Vassilis Toumazatos, Superintendent Electrician Costas Afaloniatis and Staff Captain George Douranos. Local surveyors were also employed to supervise and inspect steel construction, preservation and painting. As Costis Stamboulelis recalls, because of the other ongoing projects in four different yards, the plan approval process was complicated as indeed was the scheduling of meetings:

'All correspondence regarding drawings and calculations was addressed to our office in Kiel from where I submitted the relevant material to the Greek authorities. Plan approval was also done in Kiel, except for interior drawings which had to be reviewed and approved by Apostolos Molindris in Athens. Apostolos, his associate, Myron Vergis, and I had to travel frequently to Okpo to have meetings with the yard, with our site team and to carry out inspections. On one occasion, a very important meeting with Vergis had to take place in Germany because of his other commitments. The Koreans sent their designers to our office in HDW in order to avoid delays. Language was certainly a problem, but in most cases, the Koreans would find the right person who was able to explain to us their points and understand our requests and comments. In building the interior, they did face additional problems because they had never before worked with some of the materials specified by the architects. They were however always ready to accept when something was not done correctly and do it again by ordering new material.

Complicated and unfamiliar as our vessel was to most of them, it was still a very small ship compared with the giant oil tankers and big container ships they were building at the same time. When approaching the yard one morning, I saw the newly-completed *Blue Star Paros* lying alongside a white-painted Greek-owned VLCC and from a distance the ferry looked like the tanker's bunker vessel. The size of the yard itself was impressive – in an aerial photo of the yard and the town of Okpo, the yard occupied more space than the town. Daewoo is indeed the biggest yard I have ever visited and experienced anywhere in the world. It is a wonder of human organisational ingenuity.'

The *Blue Star Paros* was delivered in April 2002 and was placed in service between Piraeus, Paros, Naxos and Santorini. The *Blue Star Naxos* followed in June and was placed on the same popular and busy route. According to Costis Stamboulelis,

'The new Blue Star brand name and ships received an enthusiastic reception from the Greek travelling public and none of us – dare I say it not even Alexander Panagopoulos – expected such a good outcome. The people of the Cyclades islands did not refer to the ships by their names (*Ithaki, Paros, Naxos*, etc.), but by the generic name 'Blue Star' and this spread all over the country and to non-Greek passengers too. Only much later, when there were so many Blue Star Ferries in operation that travel agents issuing tickets had to ask prospective passengers which Blue Star ferry they wanted to travel on, or had to explain to them which Blue Star ferry was going to their destination, did the full names come to be widely used.'

In 2002, Superfast was operating a ten-strong fleet and Blue Star Ferries had five conventional ships plus two catamarans, while another six older conventional ferries were operating under the Blue Ferries brand with two in addition chartered out (the former *Blue Galaxy* and *Blue Island*). Altogether, Attica Enterprises had full or part ownership of no fewer than twenty-five ferries, seventeen of which were less than a decade old. In the context of a Greek ferry industry

The **Blue Star Paros** navigates amid the spectacular scenery of the Caldera at Santorini. *(Bruce Peter)*

otherwise still for the most part comprising ageing and slow vessels, the transformation brought about by Attica's involvement in the ferry sector was remarkable.

The problem of elderly tonnage had made itself horribly obvious in September 2000 when the 34-year old *Express Samina*, owned by Hellas Ferries accidentally sailed into rocks off the harbour at Paros and sank with the loss of eighty passengers. Many others were rescued by islanders who went out in their fishing boats to pluck survivors from the sea. Although the vessel's age was not so much the main factor in the disaster as were poor navigation and bridge command procedures, the rapid capsizing indicated a need to phase out vessels which would not have met current regulations had they been in service in northern Europe. The *Express Samina* tragedy proved to be an urgent wake-up call for the Greek maritime authorities and for the Greek ferry industry.

The vessel's operator, which although using Hellas Ferries as a brand, was officially known as Minoan Flying Dolphins, had been created less than two years previously as the result of an amalgamation of the fleets of several family-owned traditional Greek ferry companies. This project had been masterminded by the managing director of Minoan Lines, Pantelis Sfinias – who was also the President of the Union of Coastal Passenger Ships and Owners – and by Peter Livanos and Nicolaos Vicatos of the Ceres group of companies, which owned the Aegean Flying Dolphins passenger catamaran fleet. Finance was provided by the National Bank of Greece, Eurobank and Citibank. Their plan was radically to modernise the Aegean ferry industry – but what actually happened was that they paid high prices to buy out existing operators whose fleets were in many cases only fit for the scrapyard. The *Express Samina* had been one of a number of old ferries Hellas Ferries had inherited from Agapitos Lines; others were contributed by Lindos Lines, Poseidon Lines, Ventouris Sea Lines and the Aegean operations of Agoudimos Lines. Other than repainting with new names and logos, little else was done to any of them. In the longer term, however, the plan was to order new catamaran tonnage of the type Pericles Panagopoulos had nearly purchased from Austal back in the early-1990s. Some months after the sinking of the *Express Samina*, Pantelis Sfinias committed suicide and although the company he had co-created did indeed eventually order some new catamarans, the ramifications of the sinking handicapped it for some years and it never regained its brief initial momentum.

In the wake of Hellas Ferries' difficulties, Blue Star Ferries increasingly became a major player in the Aegean ferry market, winning public trust and market share on account of its modern, clean and punctual ships. (At around this point, Pericles and Alexander Panagopulos officially changed the spelling of their family name and the revised spelling is used henceforth.)

Soon after the *Blue Star Paros* and *Blue Star Naxos* entered service, in 2003 Costis Stamboulelis began working with his usual naval architectural collaborator, Holger Terpet of Knud E. Hansen A/S, on a design for a new class of substantially bigger ferry for domestic trade to the islands of the Cyclades and the Dodecanese. While taking into account the length limitations imposed by island ports, their aim was to increase passenger capacity and comfort, enlarge trailer lane metre capacity and enable a higher service speed. Their desire to have an upper vehicle deck suitable for loading trailers complicated the exercise as it generated a chain of new calculations and revisions in order to meet stability criteria which, in turn, had implications for power and dimension restrictions and so on.

Adding further complexity to the design process, Daewoo, the first shipyard they contacted in 2004, presented their own limitations, which had not been expected. Daewoo's intention was to build the vessels ashore – just the same as they had done with the *Blue Star Ithaki*, *Blue Star Paros* and *Blue Star Naxos* – but their track infrastructure for moving ships to the floating dock had a breadth limit of 21 metres and no more. Unfortunately, the Attica/Knud E. Hansen A/S design exceeded this by more than two metres, but nonetheless the yard was not prepared to abandon this approach. Discussions with Daewoo continued to try to reach a compromise regarding the breadth of the vessel. Eventually they conceded to allow another half metre of breath and Attica agreed to a small reduction in trailer capacity, but still it was impossible to bridge the gap between the two parties' requirements. As Costis Stamboulelis remembers,

'Sadly, we parted company without agreement. Daewoo's Mr. D. H. Park returned to Korea, but at the same time we started considering the possibility of reducing our requirements and concluded that we could live with the vessel dimensions proposed by the yard. So we asked Mr. Park to come back to Greece only to let him return to Korea just 24 hours later – still empty handed. That was a very embarrassing situation and had been caused by a sudden announcement by the Greek government regarding the control of domestic ferry operations. Mr Panagopulos was understandably very frustrated about it, saying that he was not going to make an investment and let the state run his business. From my perspective, the whole situation was most unfortunate and, making matters worse, we had damaged our good relationship with Daewoo. After the shock

The large forward-facing lounge on the ***Blue Star Naxo***s, featuring soothing colours and low partitions to engender a greater sense of intimacy in each section. *(Apostolos Molindris)*

The reception area on the **Blue Star Naxos** which, as with all of Apostolos Molindris's ferry interiors for Attica-owned ships featured comfortable seating adjacent to the counter. (*Apostolos Molindris*)

The view looking aft in the forward lounge on the **Blue Star Naxos**.
(*Apostolos Molindris*)

The same space, looking forward and showing the two-deck-high forward-facing windows covered in blinds for night-time navigation.
(*Apostolos Molindris*)

had subsided we returned to the drawing board and revised our design in the hope that the state would not implement all the controls they had announced.

With Daewoo no longer in the picture, we sent fresh enquiries to many other shipyards in Europe and South Korea. Most of the European yards were far too expensive and so we did not pursue our negotiations. Only a couple of them – namely Barreras in Spain and ENVC in Portugal – made offers we felt worth pursuing further. Barreras, located in Vigo, had valuable experience form building numerous ferries of various types for Spanish operators and was actually a good candidate for obtaining our order. Yet, in spite of taking advantage of a special Spanish tax lease scheme, it was not much less expensive than the other contenders. ENVC, on the other hand, was a small yard in Viana do Castelo with practically no experience in ferry building. We did however visit it and had a number of meetings, but at the end of every meeting their price was increased. The limited capacity of the yard, coupled with rumours about a possible change of ownership and the successive price increases were not promising signs so we decided to look elsewhere.

It was then that a new shipyard from the Far East suddenly appeared, expressing their strong interest in our project. We had never heard of the Singapore Technologies Marine Shipyard, but nonetheless its sales people appeared to know a lot about our company and our business. We discussed the project with their delegation and were pleased to see that they could accommodate our requirements. Following numerous exchanges we finally reached an agreement on price and delivery time as well as on the terms of the contract and we set a date for signing the contract in Singapore.

A big group of Attica and Blue Star executives – consisting of Alexander Panagopulos, Michael Sakellis, Michael Gialouris, Spiros Paschalis, Panagiotis Papadodimas, Maria Stamouli, my colleague George Anagnostou and myself – flew to Singapore in November 2006 for the signing ceremony – but, alas, it was not to be. When George Anagnostou and I met with the yard's designers, they opened their copy of our specification in which they had made changes and added remarks to practically every single line. There appeared to be nothing in what we had supplied that they would accept without making changes. Among all the points, they would not even accept the specified limits for noise and vibration levels which were the same as on the reference ship *Blue Star Paros* and they continued refusing

The **Blue Star Ithaki** arrives at Mykonos. *(Bruce Peter)*

even when we showed them the actual measurements made on her which were better than those in the specification we had given them to tender against. Alexander Panagopulos, Michael Gialouris and I had a private meeting with the yard's managing director and the sales director in which we were told they would not accept either our specified speed or deadweight for the vessel. We naturally told them we could have no deal under these circumstances and so we all returned home very disappointed. As it turned out, we were lucky because we would perhaps have faced the same insurmountable problems as another ferry company did a couple of years later.

In spite of the unfortunate events, we got something good out of our Singapore experience. In those days, deliveries of ships of all types depended entirely on the ability to buy engines and due to high demand there were long delays for these. Singapore Technologies' designers had done their own power/speed calculations and they kindly advised us that we would need more power and different engines than the ones we had put in the specification. For the first time ever Alex and I discussed the matter of ordering the engines ourselves before any shipbuilding contract. We decided to do it and followed the

yard's advice for increased power which proved to be correct approach.'

Before an alternative builder could be found, there were other fresh developments at Attica. in March 2003, the company strengthened its presence on the Aegean by switching the *Blue Star 2* from the Adriatic to commence instead a route from Piraeus to Chania on Crete in completion with the incumbent Cretan operator ANEK Lines. The routes from Piraeus to Crete were highly competitive, however, and ANEK – being locally-owned, long-established and dominant, continued to attract the bulk of trade, particularly lucrative agricultural cargoes as Cretan farmers had long-term contracts with it. The Blue Star Ferries service lasted only until 2005, when the *Blue Star 2* was returned to the Adriatic to operate once more alongside the *Blue Star 1*.

By this point, passengers travelling with Superfast were also able to book onward travel to the Greek islands with Blue Star Ferries at discounted fares and the two brands were marketed together as 'Premium Alliance'. This took inspiration from the global airline codeshare partnerships 'Star Alliance' and 'One World'.

CHAPTER SEVEN

ATTICA GROUP'S OTHER PROJECTS AND INVESTMENTS

I n addition to the expansion of its Superfast and Blue Star Ferries fleets, Attica Group simultaneously developed other less high profile projects.

In 2004, Attica began planning a bespoke design of ro-ro freight ship as a result of having been approached by a young Romanian naval architect, Marios-Thiera Cotletz, whose company, CMT-Engineering was based in Mangalia and who requested an appointment for a meeting with Pericles Panagopulos. He brought with him a 1:150 scale model of a highly novel combined ro-ro oil tanker vessel which could be used to replenish filling stations in the Greek islands. Although Costis Stamboulelis was intrigued by this idea, he asked that instead Cotletz should devise a pure ro-ro freight vessel measuring 5,500 gt and containing 1,300 lane metres of space in a hull measuring no more than 134 metres in length by 21 metres in breadth to enable it to pass through the Corinth Canal. An initial quotation to build Coteltz's design was received from Severnav, an old Romanian shipyard in Drobeta-Turun Severin on the Danube. The length dimension specified by Attica was subsequently increased first to about 144 metres, then to 153 metres and finally to 171.5 metres, which was too long to fit Severnav's site. Other yards in Norway, Germany, Italy, Greece, Croatia, Holland, Spain and even Ukraine were approached but no deal was concluded.

While these ultimately fruitless discussions were underway, in January 2005 Attica purchased the 5,972 gt, 1,300-lane metre freight ferries *Marin* and *Nordia* to expand cargo capacity on the Superfast Germany-Finland route. The freighters actually operated between Rostock and Uusikaupunki, a freight port where an additional ro-ro berth was available. They had been built in 1991 by Hjörungavaag Shipyard at Hjörungavaag in Norway as the *Ann-Marie* and *Bore Nordia*. In 2007 Attica acquired the broadly similar though slightly larger and newer 7,606 gt *Shield* and *Challenge*, which had been built by Astilleros de Huelva S.A. at Huelva in Spain in 1998-1999 for an Estonian owner as the *Leili* and *Lembitu*. At the time of the purchase, they were operating under charter between Britain and Ireland.

Also in 2005, Attica made opportunistic investments in other

The brand new **Nissos Chios** is seen at Piraeus in 2007. *(Bruce Peter)*

Greek ferry operators, firstly buying speculatively a 12.33 per cent shareholding in Minoan Flying Dolphins which traded under the Hellas Flying Dolphins, Hellas Ferries, Saronikos Ferries and Sporades Ferries brands in the Aegean with some routes running in competition with those of Blue Star Ferries. In the preceding two years Minoan Flying Dolphins had sold several of the older conventional ferries operated by Hellas Ferries, in some cases for scrapping but in others back to their previous private family owners who continued to operate them much as before. Their replacements were six new Kværner Fjellstrand passenger catamarans – the *Flying Cat 1-6* – plus four considerably bigger Austal vehicle-carrying catamarans, the *High-Speed 1-4*, all of which entered service in 2005. In addition, in 2004 Minoan Flying Dophins had secured from the Hellenic Shipyards at Skaramanga the incomplete conventional ferries *Superferry Mykonos* and *Superferry Chios*, which had originally been ordered by Strintzis Lines but the orders for which had been cancelled in 2002 by Attica Enterprises due to the slow progress

The *Nissos Mykonos* calls at Chios while en route between Mythilene and Piraeus. *(Bruce Peter)*

Adriatic ferries wholly and partially owned by Attica Group: the **_Superfast XI_** and Minoan Lines' **_Europa Palace_** pass each other off Ancona in 2007. *(Bruce Peter)*

The South Korean-built **_Ariadne Palace_**, pictured here off Corfu, was one of many large and speedy ro-pax ferries commissioned by Minoan Lines in the early-2000s. *(Bruce Peter)*

Its livery modified with the addition of Tallink hull and funnel markings, the **Superfast IX** is seen at Helsinki in March 2007. *(Marko Stampehl)*

being made by the yard. In the end, the two ferries were completed by subcontractors, the first at Skaramanga and the second at the Elefsis Shipyard and they entered service in 2005 and 2007 respectively as the *Nissos Mykonos* and *Nissos Chios*.

Shortly after Attica brought its shareholding in Minoan Flying Dolphins, the company's subsidiaries were consolidated and uniformly rebranded as Hellenic Seaways with an entirely new and more professional-looking visual identity to accompany the many new vessels being introduced. Perhaps predictably, this positive change was strongly encouraged by the image-conscious Alexander Panagopulos. In place of the previous all-white scheme, the new image consisted of a dark blue hull and red funnel casing with a logo featuring three dolphins, the overall impression being commensurate in terms of style and quality with Attica's two existing majority-owned ferry businesses.

Less than a month after buying its minority interest in Minoan Flying Dolphins, Attica also purchased a 10.23 per cent shareholding in the Cretan ferry operator Minoan Lines which, in addition to its core Piraeus-Heraklion (Crete) route, also ran cross-Adriatic services in competition with Superfast; all of these were operated by state-of-

The Tallink-branded **Superfast VIII** approaches Rostock in evening light in June 2011. *(Marko Stampehl)*

The laid-up **Diagoras** at Piraeus in 2006 following the failure of Dane Sea Line; Attica's purchase of the company's assets gave it ownership of this modern and recently-converted former-Japanese ferry. *(Bruce Peter)*

The laid-up and slightly-derelict **Rodos**, which Attica sold for scrapping soon after acquiring Dane Sea Line' assets. *(Bruce Peter)*

Also laid up at Keratsini near Piraeus was the **Patmo**s, which was likewise consigned for scrapping. *(Bruce Peter)*

The **Blue Star 1** departs Rosyth during a short phase in 2007-2008 operating between there and Zeebrugge; a 'Superfast' painted panel has been added to the aft hull topsides. *(Bruce Peter)*

The renovated and repainted **Diagoras** is seen at Rhodes, operating for Blue Star Ferries. *(Bruce Peter)*

The **Jean Nicoli**, ex-**Superfast X**, departs Antwerp in March 2007 at the commencement of a very brief phase in the livery of SNCM. *(Philippe Holthof)*

the-art fast ro-pax ferry tonnage built in the 1997-2006 period, either in Norway by Fosen Mekaniske Verksted, in Italy by Fincantieri or in South Korea by Samsung Heavy Industries. At the time of Attica's investment, the Minoan Lines fleet consisted of the 30,010 gt, 26.4-knot *Ikarus Palace* and *Pasiphae Palace* plus the 28,007 gt, 28.5-knot *Ariadne Palace* operating between Patras, Igoumenitsa, Corfu and Venice; the 36,825 gt, 29.5-knot *Euproa Palace* and *Olympia Palace* linking Patras, Igoumenitsa and Ancona; and the 37,482 gt, 29.5-knot *Knossos Palace* and *Festos Palace*, running between Piraeus and Heraklion. Attica's interest in Minoan Lines was soon increased to over 11 per cent and so it could now claim that, alongside its own Superfast and Blue Star Ferries brands, it was also involved in a small way in two of the other major Greek ferry businesses. Neither the investment in Hellenic Seaways nor the one in Minoan Lines lasted for long, however; as Attica was unable to expand its shareholding in Hellenic Seaways, it sold its minority stake less in January 2006, then disposed of its Minoan shares in June 2007 (there were differences of opinion within the management regarding the wisdom of this sale).

In April 2006, Attica sold the Superfast Rostock-Hanko service and the ferries *Superfast VII*, *Superfast VIII* and *Superfast IX* to the rapidly-expanding Estonian ferry operator, Tallink Grupp. As part of the agreement with Tallink, the vessels were allowed to continue sailing under the Superfast brand until the end of the following year. Attica nonetheless retained the parallel freight service between Rostock and Uusikaupunki operated by the *Marin* and *Nordia* – but in the following year it was closed down and the two vessels were briefly chartered out before being placed in Adriatic service, providing additional capacity in Superfast's 'home market' between Greece and Italy.

Next, in July 2006, Attica Enterprises bought at auction the shipping assets of a bankrupt Greek ferry operator, Dane Sea Lines, which until two years previously had operated between Piraeus and the islands of the Dodecanese. Their attraction was a recently-converted ferry bought from Japan in 2001 named the *Diagoras*. Built in 1989 by the Naikai shipyard of Setoda as the *New Tosa*, the vessel measured 6,939 gt and, following conversion, had a capacity of 1,200 passengers, 400 of whom were berthed, as well as a substantial vehicle capacity. Dane Sea Lines' two other ferries, the *Patmos* and *Rodos*, were also Japanese-built but older and in relatively poor condition and so they were consigned for scrapping. The *Diagoras*, however, was smartly renovated and returned to service under the Blue Star Ferries brand from Piraeus via Astypalea, Kalymnos and Kos to Rhodes.

In August 2006, the *Superfast X*, operating on the North Sea

The **Seafrance Molière**, ex-**Jean Nicoli**, ex-**Superfast X**, arrives at Dover in the summer of 2009. *(Bruce Peter)*

between Rosyth and Zeebrugge was sold to the French transport conglomerate Veolia with delivery early the following year as the *Jean Nicoli*; it intended that the vessel would be used as part of a bid with the French state-owned Mediterranean ferry operator, SNCM, to run a subsidised route from Marseille to Corsica, but when the bid did not win, Veolia subsequently chartered the vessel to ANEK Lines and it was returned to cross-Adriatic service, this time in competition with Superfast's own vessels of a similar type. In 2008, it was transferred to the Dover Strait ferry operator, SeaFrance, for service on the short route between Calais and Dover as the *SeaFrance Molière*. Although many of the cabins were stripped out and additional public rooms were created in their place, the vessel's constricted internal layout did not lend itself sufficiently well to short-duration, high-throughput operation. Meanwhile, to continue the Superfast service between Rosyth and Zeebrugge, in 2007 the *Blue Star 1* was deployed, unmodified except for the installation of a small number of additional passenger cabins, the provision of water traps in the big circular openings on the upper vehicle deck and the painting of large red panels on the hull topsides with the Superfast logo (but otherwise retaining the existing Blue Star Ferries livery and hull graphics).

To outside observers, it appeared to be 'business as usual' at Attica Group – albeit with Superfast now a somewhat slimmer operation than before. Within the boardroom, however, a major unexpected change was about to occur.

CHAPTER EIGHT

ATTICA GROUP IN NEW OWNERSHIP

In September 2007, Attica Group's founders, Pericles and Alexander Panagopulos, suddenly sold their 49 per cent shareholding, worth 285 million Euros, to the Greek banking and investment company, Marfin Investment Group (MIG). The reasons for them taking this decision have never been disclosed.

Following the Panagopuloses' withdrawal, there was a restructuring of the Board of Directors and it was also decided to move to a new headquarters in Athens. The new Chief Executive Officer was Peter Vettas, whose background was in chartering and bulk carrier shipping, and the Chief Financial Officer became Yannis Criticos, who had been with Attica from the time Pericles Panagopulos had first acquired it and was latterly the Line Director of the North Sea Superfast route. Under the new ownership, the Board decided to re-focus on Greek domestic operations and on the cross-Adriatic trade. Consequently, the Rosyth-Zeebrugge service operated by the *Blue Star 1* was to be closed down in September 2008 and the vessel returned to the Adriatic for use on the Patras-Igoumenitsa-Bari route. Operating on the North Sea from a headquarters in Athens while arranging crewing with Greek seafarers was a costly business and it was considered by Attica that insufficient profits were being made for the service to be worth continuing. (Subsequently, the Danish-Dutch operator Norfolkline re-opened the route, using a more freight-orientated ferry, but this too proved to be a brief interlude.)

A wider problem at that time was the cost of fuel, the existing Superfast vessels being relatively greedy when operating at speed with all four engines. In the first decade of the new century, oil prices rose sharply and this compromised the vessels' profitability. Of the original fleet, by 2008 only four examples – the *Superfast V*, *Superfast VI*, *Superfast XI* and *Superfast XII* – remained in Attica's ownership, all four linking Patras, Igoumenitsa and Ancona. The *Blue Star 1* having returned to the Mediterranean was employed in the Aegean between Piraeus and the Dodecanese.

In June 2008, however, Attica Group announced an agreement to buy from Grimaldi Holding S.p.A. of Genoa two new 25,760 gt freight-orientated ro-pax vessels under construction at the Nuovi Cantieri Apuania shipyard at Marina di Carrara in Italy. These were the fourth and the sixth of a series of eight ordered by Aldo Grimaldi – the former owner of the Grandi Navi Veloci ferry company – primarily for sale or for charter to other companies. Each could carry up to 1,000 passengers, of whom just 375 were berthed, but they had 2,623 lane metres for freight – a big increase of around 700 metres over the existing Superfast vessels. Capable of 24 knots, they were also somewhat slower and consequently less fuel-hungry but, as the intention was to operate them between Patras, Igoumenitsa and Bari, which was a shorter passage than from Ancona, this would not be problematic.

The idea of buying vessels of this type had first been investigated by Pericles Panagopulos and Costis Stamboulelis who had visited the Nuovi Cantieri Apuania shipyard in the beginning of 2007 when the *Coraggio* – the first of the series ordered by Aldo Grimaldi – was nearing completion. Panagopulos thought that the design was efficient and was interested in pursuing a deal to buy several examples – but he intended that any ordered by Attica would have a revised general arrangement in order to increase their passenger capacity. During their stay in Marina di Carrara, Panagopoulos and Stamboulelis discussed that possibility with the yard's naval architects who agreed to produce revised drawings to be presented with their offer. This was the last trip Panagopoulos and Stamboulelis made together as about a few months later Attica was sold to MIG.

When the revised design drawings eventually arrived at Attica's Athens headquarters, the new owners decided that, rather than ordering their own modified vessels, they would instead negotiate with Aldo Grimaldi to buy two out of the series he had already ordered. The deal was concluded very quickly and John Revelas and Vassilis Toumazatos were sent to the yard to supervise their construction. According to Costis Stamboulelis,

'It was a new experience for us because the building contract was between the yard and Grimaldi, whereas our contract was

The **Superfast VI** is seen berthed at Patras between crossings from and to Ancona in Italy. *(Bruce Peter)*

with Grimaldi but not the yard. Grimaldi had his own technical staff supervising the construction of the vessels, so our comments had to be submitted through their supervision team, who were all Italian. It was occasionally difficult, but in the end it did work. Although I wanted to make changes to replicate some of the established Superfast style, most of these were vetoed on account of cost.'

In the end only a small number of modifications were allowed which were considered indispensable. These included the provision of hatches in the funnel and various ducts to enable proper access to the engine room ventilation fans, the widening of the provisions hatch for loading ship's stores on pallets, the inclusion of cabins for handicapped passengers, modification of the casino, the fitment of telephones in all cabins, the addition of more CCTV cameras and the installation of an IT network.

In terms of build quality, the two completed vessels appeared less substantial than the German-built Superfasts and, inboard, their passenger accommodation, which was designed by the Italian firm, Studio di Jorio, was rather less intimate but more glitzy than had been typical of previous purpose-built Superfast tonnage. The first of the pair, which revived the name *Superfast I*, was delivered in October 2008 and the second, the *Superfast II*, entered service a year thereafter.

An aerial view of the **Superfast VI**. *(Attica Group)*

The recently-introduced Italian-built and freight-orientated second *Superfast I* approaches Patras in 2010. *(Marko Stampehl)*

As freight-carrying workhorses, however, the two proved highly effective – and profitable. They therefore reflected a more pragmatic and market-orientated approach to ferry design and specification whereas previously the personal pride of the Panagopuloses had been reflected in Superfast's bespoke ship designs. (A few years after the new *Superfast I* and *Superfast II* had been delivered a conversion proposal was prepared for the vessels to add more cabins and provide extra space in the public rooms – but this was not carried out at that time.)

In December 2008 Attica Group merged its two ferry operating subsidiaries, Superfast Ferries Maritime S.A. and Blue Star Maritime S.A., both of which were absorbed by Attica Holdings S.A. When that happened, Attica Group announces that its share capital was being almost doubled from 55,035,163 Euros to 117,539,371 Euros (representing 141,613,700 shares, valued at Euro 0.83 each). Finally, in June 2009, orders were placed for two large domestic ferries which

had been designed back in 2003 with Daewoo Shipbuilding and Marine Engineering of Okpo in South Korea at a price of 90.0 million US dollars each. The delivery of the first was scheduled for the spring of 2011 while that of the second was to occur in the first quarter of 2012.

Bringing these projects to the point of placing orders had been a complex undertaking. Following Attica's earlier disappointment in Singapore, they had established contact through their French broker with the Spanish shipyard, Astilleros de Sevilla, located on the River Guadalquivir. The yard's neglected-looking dry-dock had ample space to build a ferry of the type Attica desired and recently, it had secured an order for a new ferry from Viking Line in Finland, the construction of which would precede the potential Attica project. That way, the yard's staff would hopefully learn necessary skills before beginning work on their vessel.

All the while, Costis Stamboulelis and his colleagues continued

Onboard the new *Superfast I* and *Superfast II* had more limited passenger accommodation than the vessels they replaced, but nonetheless provided a high level of comfort. The design was by Studio DeJorio. Here, we see a lounge on the *Superfast II*. *(Bruce Peter)*

Part of the cafeteria on the *Superfast II*. (Bruce Peter)

The bar on the *Superfast II*. (Bruce Peter)

The **Superfast II** approaches Bari during the summer of 2013. *(Bruce Peter)*

A view across the **Superfast II**'s weather deck with trucks parked, en route between Igoumenitsa and Patras. *(Bruce Peter)*

working to develop their design in consort with Knud E. Hansen A/S. Unfortunately, their usual collaborator there, Holger Terpet, died suddenly after a short illness. His replacement was a younger man and self-confessed ferry enthusiast, Christian Bursche, who brought his own considerable expertise to the project.

During discussions with Astilleros de Sevilla, Knud E. Hansen A/S was in the final stage of preparing the hull form for model testing at the MARIN tank in the Netherlands. This work was presented to the yard but, as Costis Stamboulelis recalls, 'the "old guard" of the design department there had different ideas and wanted us to accept the hull form of one of the ferries they had built for Algerie Ferries some years before. Time after time and regardless of our arguments, they would keep coming back with the same proposal. Common ground was difficult to find and – combined with the awkward Spanish tax-lease funding scheme and our concern about the viability of the yard – negotiations were ended in the spring of 2007.' For Attica, this was perhaps a lucky escape and Viking Line was less fortunate as they had to cancel the order because of delays. Seven years later the vessel remained unfinished and abandoned. At that point, Attica briefly became interested in the possibility of buying and completing it for Greek domestic service. By 2014, the incomplete hull had been moved to a different shipyard, Factorias Vulcano in Vigo, and was the property of a Spanish bank which was paying Vulcano a maintenance fee to prevent

deterioration, but both the yard and the bank were eager to get rid of it as quickly as possible. The offer made by the yard to complete it according to Attica's specification was, however, too high and so the project was not pursued any further. (In the end, the vessel was purchased by the Spanish domestic ferry operator, Acciona Trasmediterranea, but has not been delivered yet at the time of writing.)

Back in late-2007 following the sudden sale by Pericles Panagopoulos of his controlling shareholding in Attica Group to MIG, the new owners quickly decided that enquiries to build the two new vessels for Blue Star Ferries should be continued and even suggested that investigations should be made into the possibility of building them in Greece. According to Costis Stamboulelis,

'We liked the idea and explained to the new CEO that our only choice was Elefsis Shipyards, where the *Nissos Chios* had recently been built with apparent success. When we looked more closely at the situation, we were quickly disillusioned. The yard had limited design capacity and, contrary to what we had assumed, it had not even been directly involved in the construction of the *Nissos Chios*, this having been entirely carried out by subcontractors using the yard's slipway, the cranes, machines and tools. Indeed, the only parts for which the yard had been responsible were the construction of the

The *Superfast XI* is seen off the berth in Ancona, framed by the town's fishing port and with the Fincantieri shipyard behind. *(Bruce Peter)*

The **Superfast II** and **Superfast VI** are seen off the port of Patras, arriving respectively from Bari and Ancona in July 2010. By the second decade of the twenty-first century, an increasing proportion of ticket sales were via the internet and so brochures, such as the one shown bottom right, became progressively fewer in number and smaller in size. *(Marko Stampehl)*

bulbous bow and the launching of the vessel. I sensed they were scared of this project and did not want to assume any responsibility for the design, although they were invited to attend the model tests we had ordered. They expected us to take responsibility for the whole design process and hand them the calculations and drawings they would have to follow to build the ship, which would also be our responsibility. To top it all, they quoted a high price which was totally unjustified. All discussions were terminated in April 2008.'

Shortly before this cessation, in February 2008 Attica decided to send a new enquiry to Daewoo in South Korea to which they replied negatively, claiming that the ferry did not fit into their product mix. At that time, the more advanced and efficient shipyards such as its Okpo facility in any case had full order books for large standardised ships and did not need to chase smaller, more complex and 'bespoke'

contracts, such as ferries.

In June 2008, however, Daewoo contacted Attica to express their continued interest in the project although they still cited the issue of it not fitting into their product mix. When they learned that model tests would be carried out at MARIN in early-July, they asked to attend and sent a four-person delegation which included a senior commercial manager and members of their Hydrodynamics Research and Development Team.

According to Costis Stamboulelis,

'The ship's speed in the tests was slightly below what we had specified and I was not happy about it. While the Knud E. Hansen designers were discussing the results with the experts of MARIN, the Korean hydrodynamicist told me privately not to worry because we could get the necessary speed with minor modifications. Indeed, MARIN suggested to run new tests using a 4.6-metre diameter propeller instead of the 4.4 m diameter stock propeller and furthermore to design a wedge ducktail. When this was done, the new tests gave us the good results we had been expecting.'

The Koreans were also happy and did not even raise the earlier point of contention regarding the hull breadth. Indeed, they had decided to build the vessels in their dry-dock, as Attica had originally desired.

Measuring 18,498 gt, the new ferries were to be notably capacious. In hulls measuring only 145.9 by 23.2 metres, they could carry 427 cars, or a combination of cars and trucks. This is achieved by there being no fewer than five car decks, the lowest two located

ahead of the engine room with a main vehicle deck above in which additional platform decks could be lowered with further car capacity in the aft two-thirds of Deck 5 above. The superstructure would contain two entire decks given over to very comfortable passenger facilities accommodating up to 2,400 in summer, designed by Molindris & Associates. There would also be extensive sheltered outdoor deck spaces. Four MAN B&W diesels would generate 32,000 kW of power, enabling a speed of 26-knots to be achieved.

By the time the contract for the two vessels was signed, Apostolos Molindris had already produced highly detailed interior designs and had even made a very accurate 3D animation 'walk through' film of the interiors for presentation to Attica's CEO, Peter Vettas, and other management executives. The animation also provided the shipyard and its subcontractors with a clear idea of what they would have to produce. The two ferries were for different routes, each with its own requirements. The first, to be named the *Blue Star Delos*, was for operation between Piraeus and Santorini making daily return trips with three calls *en route*, outwards each morning and back at night. Thus, its layout was optimized for a high-throughput of passengers with fast food dining – though also some cabins and a relaxing extra-tariff lounge. The second, the *Blue Star Patmos*, was for use on a

The **Superfast XI** is seen departing from Igoumenitsa bound for Patras in August 2008. *(Marko Stampehl)*

The interior architect, Apostolos Molindris, and his colleagues Evangelia Kintou and Maria Alibranti pose in front of a large section of superstructure for the **Blue Star Delos** at the Daewoo shipyard at Okpo. *(Apostolos Molindris collection)*

The handing-over day for the **Blue Star Patmos** with, left to right, the naval architects Chris-Alexander Korfiatis and Costis Stamboulelis, the head of Attica Group's Legal Department, Panayotis Papadodimas and its CEO, Spiros Paschalis. *(Costis Stamboulelis collection)*

longer route from Piraeus to the Dodecanese. Consequently, it needed more cabins and reclining seats both self service and a la carte restaurants.

When Attica's newbuilding team began their post-contract exchanges with Daewoo to fine-tune and agree the details of numerous plans and diagrams, they were surprised to discover that none of the engineers who had been involved in the design and building of the previous Blue Star vessels were there anymore. Every one of them had been transferred to other departments and some had even gone to other shipyards. The management had not considered it necessary to at least maintain a nucleus of people with knowledge of passenger ship construction since the delivery of the *Blue Star Naxos* in 2002. As Costis Stamboulelis recalls, 'We quickly realised that we would have to go back to basics and explain in detail and from scratch what we were aiming at and how things should be done - and this was not just confined to the interior outfitting, but concerned almost every aspect of the entire vessel.' Furthermore, in the eight years that had elapsed, the Okpo yard had grown even bigger than before and was now building mainly large container ships, drill ships and liquid natural gas carriers, but fewer large oil tankers. Attica's ferries were the only passenger ships in the order book.

Early in 2010, Attica established a site office at the yard, which was headed by John Revelas, assisted by, among others, Vassilis Toumazatos, Captain Spyros Pefanis, Superintendent Chief

Electrician Constantinos Damianakis and local surveyors for steel construction, preservation and painting. Later on, as the construction was advancing, Charalambos Nikolaides supervised the interior outfitting and the officers of the two ships joined the team. Costis Stamboulelis and his colleagues from Attica's Athens headquarters visited on a monthly basis and, in between, dealt with all of the correspondence regarding progress. In some of these frequent visits they were joined by Apostolos Molindris and some of his associates who had to make sure of the accurate implementation of approved drawings and of the appropriate use of materials selected after lengthy discussions with the yard and its subcontractors. The requirement in the specification for mock ups of the interiors to be built by the yard was a new departure in their usual production process and their subsequent inspection led both to some aggravation and amusing discussions. While cooperation was generally good and the yard's approach was professional and dedicated, according to Costis Stamboulelis,

'Their desire to do everything in-house without seeking assistance from expert consultants caused some mistakes to be made which were costly to correct. In the end, consultants were brought in after all, but it took time and many heated debates. We usually had continuous meetings to resolve various issues, so at certain points there could be between 20 and 30 people waiting for their turn outside our site office. We really came

Costis Stamboulelis (centre) and his colleagues Myron Vergis and Chris-Alexander Korfiatis at the Daewoo shipyard. *(Apostolos Molindris)*

Dressed overall with signal flags, the **Blue Star Patmos** arrives in Piraeus for the first time at the end of its long delivery voyage from South Korea in July 2012. *(Apostolos Molindris)*

very close to issuing priority tickets! All in all, it was a nerve testing project for both parties but in the end the yard displayed an exemplary performance in the delivery formalities and Attica acquired two high-quality beautiful vessels.'

For the delivery voyages to Greece, which involved passing the pirate-infested waters off Somalia and Yemen, temporary camouflage measures had to be implemented – for example, the upper garage deck side openings were sealed with plywood panels painted white so as to look from a distance like continuous steel shell plating. Similar panels were prepared to seal the front lounge deck windows.

The *Blue Star Delos* left Okpo in October 2011 under the command of Captain Pefanis. When in the sea lane south of Yemen an attempt to approach the vessel was made by a single pirate boat which quickly gave up due to the ferry's speed and instead attacked a Turkish bulk carrier which was following. Fortunately a safe arrival was made in Piraeus in early-November.

When the *Blue Star Patmos* was nearing completion in March 2012, alas, John Revelas suffered a stroke while standing on the stern ramp and he passed away a few hours later in the local hospital. The vessel left Okpo in June 2012, also under the command of Captain Pefanis, and arrived in Piraeus in July. *En route*, she encountered

persistently heavy seas and when close to Aden was approached by three pirate boats. When the speed was increased from 21 to 25.5 knots they gave up the chase, however, and another successful delivery was achieved.

Upon entering service, the *Blue Star Delos* and the *Blue Star Patmos* came quickly to be widely regarded by passengers and ferry industry observers alike as the best vessels ever seen on Greek domestic routes, offering an unprecedented level of spaciousness and comfort. In 2012, their design won a ShipPax award for its excellence – an achievement of which Attica is very proud.

While the projects to build these vessels had been under development, in the autumn of 2008, a global economic downturn began in the United States of America where unsustainable levels of debt caused a rapid loss of confidence. The suddenly difficult times spread to Europe and Greece, which had accumulated a very large debt burden, was particularly exposed. The circumstances of these events were complex and fall out with the scope of the present work but in order to reduce Greece's level of borrowing, the European Central Bank, the European Commission and the International Monetary Fund imposed a draconian regime of austerity on the country. This led to a decline of trade across the Adriatic, affecting all ferry operators there, but the domestic ferry market was less harmed as islanders still needed to commute back and forth to the mainland. Thus, in the years after 2008, Attica Group rescheduled its operations in the Adriatic and the Aegean a part of the Superfast

In morning light, the **Blue Star Delos** gathers speed off Piraeus at the commencement of a busy day of 'island hopping' among the Central Cyclades and Santorini. *(Bruce Peter)*

Upon ascending the embarkation escalators on the **Blue Star Delos** and **Blue Star Patmos** (pictured here), passengers find a three-dimensional 'WELCOME' sign which also acts as a seat and an opportunity for photographs to post on social media. *(Bruce Peter)*

Mosaic wall panelling with a 'pixelated' effect in a lounge on the **Blue Star Patmos**. *(Apostolos Molindris)*

The *Blue Star Delos* departs from Paros in the summer of 2012. *(Bruce Peter)*

The very elegant a la carte restaurant on the **Blue Star Patmos** features a wavy ceiling, covered in silver leaf. *(Bruce Peter)*

Part of the 'Goody's' fast food restaurant on the **Blue Star Delos**, showing a partition clad in a photo mural of cutlery – one of several unusual wall decorations found throughout the ship. *(Bruce Peter)*

Part of the cafeteria on the **Blue Star Patmos** with a photo mural of trees on the bulkhead and matching patterned glass partitions between the seating groups. *(Bruce Peter)*

Another view of the 'Goody's' restaurant on the **Blue Star Delos**, in which the cutlery motif is repeated on the glazed partitions. *(Bruce Peter)*

One of the toilets on the **Blue Star Patmos**, showing the precise detailing and very high standard of fit and finish achieved on board. *(Apostolos Molindris)*

An inside cabin on the **Blue Star Patmos**, offering great comfort and relaxation while the ship speeds across the Aegean. *(Apostolos Molindris)*

The 'Flo Café' for deck passengers on the **Blue Star Delos**, with an air conditioned servery area behind the glazed partition. *(Apostolos Molindris)*

The funnel of the **Blue Star Delos** at night. *(Bruce Peter)*

The **Superfast VI** approaching Patras. *(Marko Stampehl)*

fleet was sold and one vessel redeployed from the former to the latter. (This development was also a consequence of the delivery of *Superfast I* and *Superfast II*.) In March 2009 Attica re-entered the Cretan ferry market, this time by introducing the *Superfast XII*, cascaded from the Adriatic, on the Piraeus-Heraklion route in competition with the established service provided by Minoan Lines and ANEK Lines. Just over a year later, a second Cretan service was begun between Piraeus and Chania under the Blue Star Ferries brand and using the *Blue Horizon* in competition with ANEK Lines' vessels. In 2011, Attica and ANEK Lines agreed to pool their resources both on the Adriatic and on the route to Crete and so a three-year joint venture, ANEK-Superfast, was negotiated to cover the Patras-Ancona route and the Piraeus-Heraklion route. In 2014 the ANEK-Superfast joint venture was enhanced by jointly operating all the Adriatic and Cretan routes.

So far as sales of ships were concerned, in December 2009, the *Superfast V* was sold to a subsidiary of Brittany Ferries with delivery in the new year; henceforth, the vessel operated under the French flag as the *Cap Finisterre* across the Bay of Biscay between Portsmouth and Santander. *Superfast VI* was sold in June 2013 to a subsidiary of the Malaysian and Hong Kong-headquartered gaming conglomerate Genting for use as a shuttle vessel between Miami and a new casino resort at Bimini on the Bahamas. Renamed *Bimini Superfast*, the vessel operated for only two years before being sold back into Mediterranean ferry service, passing to Grimaldi Lines and

The *Cap Finisterre* of Brittany Ferries, ex-*Superfast V*, with a rebuilt funnel to accommodate an installation of exhaust gas scrubbers. *(Miles Cowsill)*

The *Stena Superfast VII*, formerly the *Superfast VII*, approaches Loch Ryan towards the end of a crossing from Belfast early in 2013. *(Bruce Peter)*

The Polish Unity Line's *Skandia*, ex-*Superfast I*, at Ystad in 2012. *(Bruce Peter)*

The *Atlantic Vision*, previously the *Superfast IX*, operating under charter from Tallink to Marine Atlantic between Cape Breton and Newfoundland in Canada. *(Marko Stampehl)*

Corsica Ferries' **Mega Express Four,** originally the **Superfast II**, is seen departing from Bastia, bound for Nice. Note that the superstructure has been extended aft to enclose the stern. *(Bruce Peter)*

The **Bimini Superfast**, ex-**Superfast VI**, shown while briefly operating between 2013 and 2016 for a subsidiary of the Genting casino group between Miami and the gaming resort of Bimini in the Caribbean. *(Ferry Publications Library)*

A more recent image of the same vessel as Grimaldi Lines' **Cruise Olbia**, back in the Mediterranean and linking Livorno in Italy with Olbia on Sardinia. *(Rob de Visser)*

The **Stena Superfast X**, originally the **Superfast X** and subsequently the **Jean Nicoli**, **Seafrance Molière** and **Dieppe Seaways**, approaches Dublin at the end of a crossing of the Irish Sea from Holyhead. *(Miles Cowsill)*

becoming the *Cruise Olbia* for operation between Livorno and Olbia as from March 2016.

Following these sales, only two original Superfast vessels remained in the Attica fleet– the *Superfast XI* and the *Superfast XII*. The former remained in the Patas-Igoumenitsa-Ancona route in the joint operation with ANEK whilst the latter operated in the Dodecanese route. Otherwise, Superfast's only other route is between Patras, Igoumenitsa and Bari, operated by the freight-orientated ro-pax ferries *Superfast I* and *Superfast II*.

Of the Superfast Ferries sold in the years before the 2008 downturn, the three acquired by Tallink in 2006 have all since been re-sold or chartered out. In 2008, the *Superfast IX* was taken under charter by the Canadian east coast ferry operator Marine Atlantic for service on the exposed and challenging route linking North Sydney on Cape Breton Island and Port Aux Basques in Newfoundland as the *Atlantic Vision*. Subsequently, in 2011, the *Superfast VII* and *Superfast VIII* were chartered to Stena Line for service between Cairnryan and Belfast as the *Stena Superfast VII* and *Stena Superfast VIII*. For this relatively short daytime service, a large number of their cabins were removed and the spaces converted into additional public rooms. So thorough were these modifications, which even involved cutting larger windows in the shell plating, that users would find it hard to imagine that they had ever been long-haul overnight vessels. Stena

Line is, of course, well-known throughout the ferry industry for the ingenuity of its technical staff in making radical conversions of existing tonnage. The changes also demonstrate the inherent flexibility of the underlying design.

Of the original Superfast pair, the former *Superfast I*, later *Eurostar Roma* of Grimaldi Lines, has since 2008 operated under the Polish flag on the southern Baltic between Swinoujscie in Poland and Ystad in Sweden as the *Skania* of Unity Line. The former *Superfast II*, later *Spirit of Tasmania III*, has since 2006 been operated by Corsica and Sardinia Ferries between Italian and French ports and those in Corsica as the *Mega Express Four*. An extension of the superstructure has been added towards her stern to enable 1,965 passengers to be carried, 909 of whom are berthed. This rebuild also demonstrates another aspect of flexibility in being able to extend the accommodation to give a much greater overnight capacity.

Thus, under subsequent owners, the careers of former members of the Superfast fleet have been very diverse and, following conversion and repainting in a multitude of other operators' liveries, they have taken on a wide variety of new identities. Nonetheless, their distinctive hull lines and funnels reveal that once they were members of the Ferrari red fleet which from the mid-1990s onwards transformed ferry travel across the Adriatic and elsewhere.

CHAPTER NINE

THE PURCHASE OF HELLENIC SEAWAYS AND OTHER RECENT DEVELOPMENTS

In 2012, Peter Vettas announced his decision to step down from the post of CEO de to health reasons, taking instead the post of non-executive Chairman of the Board. At that time Kyriakos Mageiras was appointed as Executive Vice Chairman and Spiros Paschalis became CEO of the company. Paschalis has been with Attica since 1996. Following the death of Peter Vettas in April 2013, Kyriakos Mageiras was appointed as Attica's new Chairman.

In recent years, Attica Group has continued to modify its fleet profile to be appropriate for current market conditions and prepared when a lucrative investment or sales opportunity emerges.

In October 2014, Attica sold the 14-year-old *Blue Star Ithaki* – the pioneer new building of Blue Star Ferries – to the Canadian government for operation between Digby in Nova Scotia and St John in Newfoundland as the *Fundy Rose*. In the following April, an agreement was made with a Greek leasing company whereby Attica would charter the 13,403 gt former-*Lefka Ori* of ANEK Lines to operate on the joint Blue Star Ferries and ANEK Piraeus-Chania service to Crete. The vessel dated from 1992 and had been built in Japan by Mitsubishi Heavy Industries as the *Hercules* for Japanese domestic service. Capable of 24 knots and with a capacity of 1,750 lane metres for cars and freight, she was ideal for the route. For Blue Star Ferries, she was renamed the *Blue Galaxy*.

An entirely new venture for Attica Group began in 2016 when it entered into a joint agreement with the Moroccan-headquartered Bank of Africa (BMCE) to commence a new ferry service between Spain and Morocco, named Africa-Morocco Link (or AML for short). The vast movement of nearly three and a half million persons of North African origin from Europe each holiday season is known in Spain as 'Operación del Estrecho' and usually involves the chartering of a great many diverse and often ageing ferries. In addition, throughout the year, there is a continuous flow of truck and car traffic across the Strait of Gibraltar between the ports of Algeciras in Spain and Tangier Med near Tangiers in Morocco. Again, this is

mostly carried on older vessels and, in recent years, several of these have become so mechanically degraded as either to have needed very costly refits or been fit only for scrapping.

It was in this context that Attica spotted an opportunity with a Moroccan partner to offer a better quality of service – albeit not of anything like the same level as provided by its Superfast or Blue Star Ferries brands. The ferries selected to inaugurate Africa-Morocco Link's Algeciras-Tangier Med service in the summer of 2016 were both well-known in Greece, being Blue Star Ferries' *Diagoras* and ANEK Lines' very large 38,261 gt *El Venizelos*, the latter of which was briefly chartered between June and September. A permanent vessel, however, was soon found from a third Greek-owned ferry company, European Seaways, which ran a budget service across the Adriatic between Igoumenitsa and Brindisi and Valona and Brindisi, usually with a different ship each season as it was more profitable to sell the existing vessel once the summer tourist rush was over. Thus, in December 2016, Africa-Morocco Link bought that year's European Seaways ferry which was the 16,071 gt *Prince*, a vessel with a remarkable history that began in 1980 when it was built at Nakskov in Denmark as a high-capacity train ferry named the *Prins Joachim* for the Danish State Railways hourly service across the Great Belt. When the Danish government completed a bridge and tunnel to replace the ferries there, after some years in lay-up, the vessel was converted into a car and truck ferry for a route between Gedser in southern Denmark and Rostock in Germany, where it subsequently shared the same port as Superfast's vessels operating to Finland and Sweden. This continued until the early-summer of 2016 when the vessel was bought by European Seaways and very quickly converted for just a few months of operation between Greece and Italy. When Africa-Morocco Link bought the *Prince*, as she was by then known, she was found to be in very good condition – a consequence of the high-level of specification demanded by her original railway owner. After repainting, upgrading, renaming as the *Morocco Star*, and re-

The **Blue Star Delos** and the **Blue Star Patmos** are seen leaving Piraeus in morning light in 2018. *(Bruce Peter)*

The **Morocco Star**, originally the Danish train and car ferry **Prins Joachim**, in the livery of Attica's Africa Morocco Link subsidiary at Algeciras. *(Matthew Murtland)*

The **Diagoras** of Blue Star Ferries operating temporarily for Africa Morocco Link across the Strait of Gibraltar in 2016. *(Matthew Murtland)*

A Piraeus Great Harbour scene in 2012 showing one of Hellenic Seaways' newest ferries, the **Nissos Mykono**s, and its oldest, the **Express Pegasus**. *(Bruce Peter)*

The Japanese-built **Nissos Rodos** of Hellenic Seaways approaches Mykonos while en route to the Dodecanese islands in 2018. *(Bruce Peter)*

Another Hellenic Seaways ferry of Japanese origin, the **Nissos Samos**, is seen at Piraeus. *(Bruce Peter)*

With the purchase of Hellenic Seaways, Attica Group also gained control of short-duration local services, such as those from Piraeus to Aegina, operated by smaller ferries, such as the Greek-built **Artemis** – but these were quickly sold. *(Bruce Peter)*

registering under the Moroccan flag, she entered service across the Strait of Gibraltar in April 2017.

To provide additional summer capacity, in 2018 Africa-Morocco Link chartered from European Seaways the 10,553 gt *Galaxy*, a vessel originally built in Poland in the late-1970s as the *Silesia* of the state-owned Polferries. Other Greek-owned conventional ferries and fast craft have also been used for brief spells to handle the large numbers of passengers traversing in summer.

Back on Attica Group's more familiar territory of the Aegean, a major achievement in 2017-2018 was its successful take-over of the biggest Greek domestic ferry operator, Hellenic Seaways. In winning a majority in the company, Attica managed to beat off the Italian Grimaldi Group, the expansion and consolidation of which had been rapid in recent years. Indeed, using profits earned in deep-sea container and ro-ro freight shipping, since the millennium, Grimaldi had built up a vast pan-European ferry network of the type the Panagopuloses had probably once envisaged for Superfast. As well as ferries operating under its own Grimaldi Lines brand in the western Mediterranean, it had bought the Baltic Sea operator Finnlines and, in 2008, an 85 per cent interest in the Cretan-headquartered Greek ferry operator, Minoan Lines, with routes both in the Adriatic and Aegean seas.

Through Minoan Lines, Grimaldi Group already effectively controlled a third of Hellenic Seaways' shares. Grimaldi was keen to increase its interest in Hellenic Seaways but was unable to persuade investors to sell enough shares to enable it to gain a majority interest. It seemed that the Greeks were unwilling to see a large part of their domestic ferry network fall into foreign ownership.

In August 2017, Attica bought out the shareholding of Piraeus Bank in Hellenic Seaways and those of other minor shareholders, amounting to 39,039,833 shares, for just over 74 million Euros (50.3%). Shortly after, in October, Attica negotiated with Minoan Lines and its parent company, Grimaldi Group, to buy 37,667,504 Hellenic Seaways shares, representing 48.53% of the share capital, for 78.5 million Euros. As part of the deal, Attica sold to Minoan

The Austal-built catamaran ferry **Highspeed 4,** one of a number of such craft in the Hellenic Seaways fleet, is seen off Piraeus. *(Bruce Peter)*

Lines and Grimaldi Lines the Austal-built catamaran High Speed 7 for 25 million Euros and *Superfast XII* for 74.5 million Euros. The former became Minoan's Santorini Palace and was placed in service between Crete and Santorini, giving a fast connection across the southern Aegean. The *Superfast XII*, meanwhile, was moved to the western Mediterranean as the *Cruise Ausonia*, joining the former *Superfast VI* in the Italy-Sardinia trade. With these deals ratified – and approved by the Greek Competition Authorities, subject to some minor operational changes at Blue Star Ferries – Attica Group now controlled a very large part of the Greek domestic ferry fleet.

The take-over of Hellenic Seaways added to Attica Group's fleet an additional seventeen conventional ferries and fast ferries. Among these were the *Nissos Mykonos* and *Nissos Chios* which Strintzis Lines had originally ordered and which, had they been built to schedule, would have become members of the Blue Star Ferries fleet. Other significant vessels, such as the 13,597 gt *Ariadne*, the 29,733 gt *Nissos Rodos* and the 19,796 gt *Nissos Samos*, were all built in Japan in the late-1980s and early-1990s and were converted in Greece in the early-2000s. With nine Blue Star Ferries plus three Superfast vessels besides, the Attica Group ferry fleet currently numbers 29 ships. Since the mid-1990s, it has grown from a single vessel – the *Superfast I*

The funnel casing of Hellenic Seaways' **Ariadne**, a converted Japanese-built ferry currently operating mostly under charter to other operators. *(Bruce Peter)*

– into one of the largest and most modern ferry companies in the world.

Future plans

At the time of going to press, Attica Group is focusing on further consolidation and also – very importantly – on attending to environmental issues and green technologies. Already on the *Blue Star Delos*, for example, part of the electrical energy is supplied by solar panels. Attica is also participating actively in EU funded projects such as the Poseidon Med II aiming at developing dual-fuel propulsion plants, while cooperating at the same time with LNG suppliers to help establish a reliable infrastructure for the efficient bunkering of its vessels. Attica's investigations are not limited only to alternative fuels, but extend to all novel solutions for energy saving from relatively simple ones, such as using silicon bottom paints, to the more complicated, such as the possibility of installing rotor sails.

The Hellenic Seaways monohulls, catamarans and hydrofoils of various types also form part of the development agenda and these light craft on shorter but very busy routes give opportunities to implement new and novel ideas which would not apply to the bigger conventional vessels.

Commercial ambitions are often constrained by the less than ideal Greek and Italian port infrastructure, which Attica has always desired to assist in improving.

Currently, Attica is working on developing three different potential future ferry types:

A day ro-pax ferry for shorter domestic routes and small ports

A compact ro-pax ferry with enhanced garage capacity within strict dimension limitation for both domestic and short international trading

A very large ro-pax ferry with more than double garage capacity as that of the existing Superfasts for international trading

All of these designs are at an advanced stage, but changes are made almost continuously so as to achieve the optimum size, form, power and equipment to guarantee the most efficient, economical and environmentally friendly operation.

As we have seen, Attica Group is an ambitious and innovative company and these characteristics underpinning its past and current successes appear set to continue into the future.

The funnel of the **Blue Star Patmos**.
(Bruce Peter)

APPENDIX - KEY MEMBERS OF THE ATTICA NEWBUILDING TEAM

Costis Stamboulelis

Having studied Naval Architecture at Sunderland Polytechnic and the University of Michigan, where he obtained his MSE, he worked until 1981 at the Advanced Technology Centre in Athens as a students' counsellor, at the Greek Tourism Organisation (EOT) as a consultant on the design of floating breakwaters and at the Technical University of Athens as a member of a team preparing a network of yacht marinas in Greece.

He was employed by Royal Cruise Line in the beginning of 1981 and was appointed as Superintendent Naval Architect to work initially on the conversion in Greece of the *Doric* into the *Royal Odyssey*. He actively participated in the design of the subsequent cruise ship newbuilding project for the *Crown Odyssey* and in the negotiations with shipyards. When the order for the vessel was placed with Meyer Werft, he was promoted to Newbuilding Project Manager at the head of the site office in Papenburg.

In 1990 following the sale of Royal Cruise Line, he became Attica Enterprises' Director of Operations, New Projects and Development. In this capacity he was responsible for preparing all the Superfast and Blue Star specifications and drawings, cooperating with consultant naval architects and interior designers and subsequently negotiating with the shipyards involved either in Europe or in Asia.

He headed Attica's supervision team for all new buildings, travelling constantly between Finland, Germany, Holland, Greece and South Korea. He was elected to the Board of Directors of Attica Group in 1999 and held this position until 2012.

He initiated the improvement of port facilities and worked closely with consultants presenting proposals for new piers, link spans, passenger terminals and traffic control to port authorities. He participated in several ship inspections, aiming to find suitable vessels for the company's expansion plans.

He is presently Attica's Executive Management Adviser for Newbuildings and Development.

John Revelas

He was an experienced naval architect and a talented draftsman. He combined his theoretical knowledge with his hands-on involvement in many cruise ship conversion projects in Greece prior to joining the Superfast supervision team and attending the construction of *Superfast III* and *Superfast IV* in Turku. His responsibility initially included the review of steel and outfitting drawings, followed by supervision and inspections of the construction in progress. He continued the same work in HDW until he was appointed to supervise the repair of *Superfast III* in Blohm and Voss. He was subsequently appointed as Head of Attica's site offices at the Hellenic Shipyards in Scaramanga and subsequently performed similar roles at Apuania and twice in Daewoo twice. In the periods between new buildings he attended regular dry-dockings of the Superfast and Blue Star Ferries vessels and supervised all minor conversions to them.

Mike Kardasis

He started his career as a naval architect in a tanker owning company. Desiring all-round knowledge of his subject, he also spent part of his tenure as a member of the crews of tankers. He was employed by Attica as a Superintended Engineer shortly after the orders for the *Superfast I* and *Superfast II* were placed and he joined the supervision team in Bremerhaven. He continued with the supervision team in Turku, Kiel and in Lübeck. He was involved in plan approval and inspections during construction. He resigned from Attica in 2001 and presently he is employed by Lloyd's Register of Shipping based in Piraeus.

Xenofon Plataniotis

He had a seagoing career as a Chief Engineer in various types of vessels - the last one being a small cruise ship of Sun Line – before joining the Attica supervision team as a Superintendent Engineer in Bremerhaven for the construction of *Superfast I* and *Superfast II*. He subsequently attended the construction of all the Superfasts in Turku,

Kiel and Lübeck. Later on, he also made a number of visits to Daewoo during the construction of *Blue Star Delos* and *Blue Star Patmos*.

He was responsible for developing with the yards the detailed machinery specification of all the vessels, reviewing all plans and piping diagrams, supervising and inspecting all installations on board and verifying performance during dock and sea trials. Another important part of his work was to attend factory tests of all major machinery prior to their dispatch to the yards.

Myron Vergis

He is an electrical engineer who started his career in shipping and acquired a great deal of valuable experience through his active participation in the completion in Perama in the early-1990s of the ANEK Lines ferry *El. Venizelos*. He was employed by Royal Cruise Line as a Superintendent Electrician and Chief Electrician on the *Crown Odyssey* where he became acquainted with the advanced automation and electrical installations on the ship. Thereafter, following the sale of the company by Pericles Panagopoulos, he worked as a Superintendent Electrician for Kloster Cruise International owners until 1997 when he joined the Superfast supervision team for the construction of *Superfast III* and *Superfast IV* in Turku. He has since then been very much involved in all Attica's new buildings, for which he developed the electrical and automation specification, reviewed the electrical plans, supervised and inspected the electrical installations and verified their performance during dock and sea trials. Although stationed firstly in Turku and then in Kiel, he travelled often to various destinations in Europe and in Asia to attend factory tests. Concurrently with Superfast's new building programme, he assumed the same responsibility also for the Blue Star new buildings in Daewoo twice – first in 2001 – 2002 and subsequently in 2010 - 2012.

As automation, monitoring and warning alarms are vital electrical systems in modern ship design, his deep involvement in discussions with the shipyards and the system suppliers were important and these continued during the implementation and final testing phases. He attended sea trials of all the Superfasts and the Korean built Blue Stars, paying particular attention to the performance of safety related installations, automation, blackout tests and other tests required for meeting Flag and Class notation requirements.

George Anagnostou

Having studied naval architecture at the University of Michigan and Ocean Engineering at the Massachusetts Institute of Technology, where he gained his PhD, he worked as a superintendent engineer in a Greek tanker company for three years and then in the design office of the Elefsis Shipyard prior to being employed by Attica. He joined the Superfast supervision team in HDW during the construction of *Superfast V* and *Superfast VI*. He assumed a central role in the coordination with the yard and participated in the final meetings leading to the delivery of the vessels. He assumed a more active role in Flender Werft during the construction of *Superfast XI* and *Superfast XII* having been appointed Head of the site office at the yard. At the same time, he attended the operation of the Baltic Superfasts during the guarantee period. He participated in the sea trials of the HDW and Flender built Superfasts with particular attention to shaft power measurements, engine performance, ventilation and vibration levels, among others.

Prior to leaving the company he was involved in the development of new company plans and in this respect he participated in various ship inspections in Europe and in Asia as well as in discussions with shipyards. He left the company in 2008 to be employed by a Greek company with a tanker construction programme in China and South Korea. He returned to Attica in 2015 and was appointed as Technical Director, succeeding John Skoutas.

John Skoutas

A Chief Engineer of bulk carriers, he was the Technical Manager of a Greek bulk carrier company for a number of years before being employed as Technical Manager of Magna Marine.

Upon delivery of *Superfast I* and *Superfast II* he was transferred to Attica as Technical Manager – later Technical and Operations Director – until 2015 when he retired. In the newbuilding programme, he coordinated reviews of plans submitted by shipyards and participated in negotiations with various machinery and equipment makers. He attended the sea trials of some of the new buildings both in Europe and in South Korea.

Chris-Alexander Korfiatis

He is one of the two young naval architects who joined the Superfast supervision team in the autumn of 1999 and stayed on site until the completion of all the German-built Superfasts, initially in HDW and subsequently at Flender.

Before coming to Attica he was a supervisor of tanker construction in Daewoo for a Greek company. While a member of the Superfast supervision team, he was involved with most aspects of the vessels under construction, reviewing plans and carrying out inspections. He attended all sea trials. Shortly after the Superfast newbuilding programme was completed, he was employed as Superintendent Engineer in a Greek cruise company. He came back to Attica as Deputy Technical Manager in 2009 and participated in the construction of *Blue Star Delos* and *Blue Star Patmos*, regularly visiting Daewoo and attending sea trials.

When *Superfast VI* was sold to Genting, he left Attica to join the operator in Miami. After a short spell he was employed by Royal Caribbean International as Associate Vice President Technical Operations.

John Speis

He is the other young naval architect who joined the Superfast supervision team in the autumn of 1999. He also stayed in Germany until the completion of all of the Superfasts built by HDW and Flender. Before coming to Attica he had worked as a Superintendent Engineer in a Greek bulk carrier company.

While in the Attica supervision team he had the same tasks as C.A. Korfiatis. He stayed in Attica as a Superintendent Engineer in charge of various conversions including the addition of new cabins in the two North Sea Superfasts in the Fosen shipyard. He left Attica in 2006 to work first in a tanker company, followed by a bulk carrier company. He is presently Technical Manager in a Greek container shipping company.

ACKNOWLEDGEMENTS

The author especially wishes to thank Costis Stamboulelis for his outstanding assistance in the writing of this book and Miles Cowsill of Ferry Publications for publishing the book. In addition, the author and publisher wish to thank Jonathan Boonzaier; Mitchell Bruce; Krystof Brzoza; Christian Bursche; Rob de Visser; Ann Glen; Rimbert Harpain; Anne Hayns; Philippe Holthof; Rob de Visser; Elspeth Hough; Søren Lund Hviid; Kalle Id; Apostolos Kaknis; Mike Louagie; Elizabeth Mandersson; Fotis Marinelis; Fanny Mavraganis; John May; Lizette May; Apostolos Molindris; Matthew Murtland; Nicholas Oddy; Spiros Paschalis; Spiros Pefanis; John Peter; René Taudal Poulsen; Ariadne Psimara; Michalis Sakellis; Richard Seville; Hercules Simitsidellis; Marko Stampehl; Dionissis Theodoratos; Myron Vergis and Tage Wandborg.